2000
FORMULA ONE
YEARBOOK

THE ESSENTIAL GUIDE TO
THE GRAND PRIX YEAR

A DORLING KINDERSLEY BOOK

Dorling DK Kindersley

LONDON, NEW YORK, SYDNEY, DELHI, PARIS, MUNICH, AND JOHANNESBURG

Produced for Dorling Kindersley by Grant Laing Partnership,
48 Brockwell Park Gardens, London SE24 9BJ

Editorial director   Reg Grant
Design director   Ruth Shane
Text   Adrian Gilbert
Additional text   Reg Grant
Picture research   Jo Walton

DORLING KINDERSLEY
Publisher   Mike Edwards
Art director   Carole Ash
Managing editor   Sharon Lucas
Senior editor   Edward Bunting
Production Sarah Coltman, Sarah Dodd

UK ISBN 0-7513-0802-1
Printed in Italy by L.E.G.O.

see our complete catalogue at
www.dk.com

CONTENTS

PRE-SEASON REVIEW

THE 2000 SEASON

FEATURES

PRE-SEASON REVIEW

McLaren: Struggling to stay in front

NO ONE DOUBTS THAT IN THE 2000 season McLaren-Mercedes will once again be the team to beat. The McLaren car looks certain to be the fastest in the contest, and Mika Hakkinen, with two consecutive drivers' championships under his belt, is thirsting for his hat-trick.

Fast but unreliable

Yet McLaren had a surprisingly nervous and untidy season in 1999. The speed of their car in qualifying guaranteed them a string of pole positions – 11 for Hakkinen in 16 grand prixs. But when it came to racing, both the car and the drivers revealed a remarkable fallibility.

A combination of mechanical failures and driver errors allowed Ferrari to beat McLaren in the constructors' championship and restrict them to a narrow victory in the drivers' championship – in spite of Michael Schumacher's injury that should, in principle, have gifted McLaren both trophies.

The 1999 season showed a new side of world champion Hakkinen. He was revealed as more emotional and less cool under pressure than his

reputation suggested. He twice crashed out when in the lead, at Imola and Monza, and at times his frustration and unhappiness were plainly visible. Yet he pulled himself together and delivered a faultless performance when it was needed to win the final grand prix in Japan and the drivers' championship.

Hakkinen's relationship with team-mate David Coulthard was a subject of debate throughout the season. McLaren insist that the two drivers must be allowed to compete, but this proved costly at the A1 Ring, where Hakkinen was spun off by Coulthard as the Scottish driver fought his colleague for the lead.

Make or break

Coulthard resents being cast in the support role, but he won only two grand prixs in 1999 to the Finn's five. Determined to improve this year, he told journalists: "I still think I can do a better job." If he fails to deliver this season, McLaren may look for a replacement. For the moment, though, innovation has been limited to the arrival of Olivier Panis as test driver.

Team Profile

Team principal Ron Dennis is one of the most thoughtful figures in the sport.

Technical director Adrian Newey is the brain behind the best car in F1.

West-McLaren-Mercedes

Team Principal . . . . .Ron Dennis
Technical Director . . . . .Adrian Newey
Mercedes-Benz
Motorsport Director . . . .Norbert Haug
Address
McLaren International Ltd, Kingsway Business Park, Albert Drive, Woking, Surrey, GU21 5JY, UK
Internet
www.mclaren.co.uk

The Car

Chassis . . . . .McLaren MP4/15
Engine . . . . .2000 Mercedes F0110J V10
Power . . . . .840 bhp
Tyres . . . . .Bridgestone

Results to end of 1999

GP Debut . . . . .GP Monaco 1966
GP Points 2327.5
GP Victories 123

Mika Hakkinen (car no. 1), left, born 28 September 1968 in Helsinki, Finland. F1 debut in the USA in 1991; to end of 1999, 128 starts, 14 wins.

David Coulthard (car no. 2), born 27 March 1971 in Twynholm, Scotland. F1 debut in Spain in 1994; to end of 1999, 90 starts, 6 wins.

Ferrari: Still waiting after all these years

THE FERRARI TEAM SHOULD have felt triumphant at the end of the 1999 season, carrying off the much coveted constructors' trophy for the first time since 1983. But there was an unmistakeable sense of frustration in the Maranello camp. The drivers' championship had once more eluded them, by a mere two points. It is now 21 years since Ferrari last won the drivers' trophy, and the long wait for victory increasingly rankles.

Staying the course

Ferrari's great strength in 1999 was reliability. They completed almost nine-tenths of their races, with Eddie Irvine suffering only one retirement in 16 starts. This gave them the edge in points over McLaren, whose car was faster but distinctly less reliable.

Ferrari's other trump card was Michael Schumacher – until a leg injury sustained at the British Grand Prix ruined his season. The brilliance of the German was undeniable. He scored 44 points in spite of missing seven races. Yet he was criticized by Ferrari boss Luca Di Montezemolo for being slow to return to the fray after his injury, reflecting doubts about his commitment to the team, as opposed to his interest in proving himself the world's greatest living driver.

Close to winning

In Schumacher's absence, his team-mate Eddie Irvine came close to winning the drivers' championship. But the outspoken Irishman was constantly at odds with the Ferrari management and unhappy with playing second fiddle to Schumacher. He predictably departed for Jaguar at the end of the season.

Irvine's replacement is Brazilian driver Rubens Barrichello, who has yet to win a grand prix in 113 starts. He has been promised that he will not have to give way to his German colleague. Whether Schumacher accepts this line remains to be seen.

Ferrari will be hoping that this year's F1-2000 model proves as reliable as last season's car – if possible with the addition of a little extra speed.

Team Profile

Team principal Luca Di Montezemolo (right) and Ferrari technical supremo Ross Brawn look optimistic at the launch of this year's car.

Michael Schumacher (car no. 3), born 3 January 1969 in Kerpen, Germany. F1 debut in Belgium in 1991; to end of 1999, 128 starts, 35 wins.

Rubens Barrichello (car no. 4), born 23 May 1972 in Sao Paulo, Brazil. F1 debut in South Africa in 1993; to end of 1999, 113 starts, no wins.

Scuderia Ferrari Marlboro

Team Principal . . Luca Di Montezemolo
Technical Director . . . . Ross Brawn
Sporting Director . . . . Jean Todt
Address
Ferrari SpA, Via Ascari 55-57, 41053
Maranello, Modena, Italy
Internet
www.ferrari.it

The Car

Chassis . . . . Ferrari F1-2000
Engine . . . . Ferrari V10 049
Power . . . . 800+ bhp
Tyres . . . . Bridgestone

Results to end of 1999

GP Debut . . . . GP Monaco 1950
GP Points 2354.5
GP Victories 125

Jordan: Building on last year's success

Team Profile

Benson & Hedges
Jordan-Mugen-Honda

Team Principal . . . . . . .Eddie Jordan
Technical Director . .Mike Gascoyne

Address
Jordan Grand Prix, Silverstone, Towcester,
Northamptonshire, NN12 8JT, UK

Internet
www.f1jordan.com

The Car

Chassis . . . . .Jordan EJ10
Engine . . . . .Mugen-Honda
MF301HE V10
Power . . . . .770+ bhp
Tyres . . . . .Bridgestone

Results to end of 1999

GP Debut . . . . .GP USA 1991
GP Points 216
GP Victories 3

EDDIE JORDAN WAS PROBABLY THE happiest team owner in Formula One at the end of the 1999 season. His team not only achieved its highest ever placing in the constructors' championship, coming third, but did so in style, 25 points clear of fourth-placed Stewart. At one point it even seemed that Jordan's Heinz-Harald Frentzen might make a challenge for the drivers' trophy; he ended up, like the Jordan team, in third place.

Honda brush-off

Given his team's high performance, Eddie Jordan must have been bitterly disappointed at Honda's decision to give their new work's engine for the 2000 season to struggling BAR, leaving Jordan with an upgrade of their Mugen-Honda. If the work's Honda proves as powerful as expected, it could have given Jordan a serious chance of challenging the dominance of McLaren and Ferrari. As it is, they will probably continue to compete to be "best of the rest", hoping to hold off the challenge of Jaguar and Williams and stay in third place. Frentzen will be looking to continue

Jordan have been promised an upgraded Mugen-Honda engine this year, but it may fail to make their car any more competitive than in 1999.

his excellent form of 1999. He will have a new partner in Italian driver Jarno Trulli, transferred from Prost. Last season the hapless Damon Hill offered Frentzen neither support nor competition. Some observers believe that the presence of the ambitious Trulli, tipped as a possible future F1 champion, could adversely affect Frentzen. But it must enhance the Jordan team's chances of a good placing in the constructors' table to have both their drivers hot for success.

Team leader *Eddie Jordan flanked by his drivers, Heinz-Harald Frentzen, left, and Jarno Trulli. Frentzen (car no. 5), born 18 May 1967 in Mönchengladbach, Germany. F1 debut in Brazil in 1994; to end of 1999, 97 starts, 3 wins. Trulli (car no. 6), born 13 July 1974 in Pescara, Italy. F1 debut in Australia in 1997; to end of 1999, 45 starts, no wins.*

Jaguar: High ambition in racing green

FEW RACING ENTHUSIASTS ARE insensitive to the romance of the Jaguar name. Yet the replacement of Stewart Grand Prix by Jaguar Racing this season owed nothing to sentiment or emotion and everything to the calculations of Ford marketing men, who believe that a winning Formula One team in British racing green is just what the Jaguar marque needs to boost its worldwide sales.

After two lean years, the team created by former world champion driver Jackie Stewart and his son Paul had at last got off the ground in 1999, edging ahead of Williams to take fourth place in the constructors' table with 36 points. Johnny Herbert gave them their first Formula One victory, when treacherous conditions decimated the field in the European Grand Prix at the Nürburgring.

Stewart steps down

But by that time Jackie Stewart had already sold out to engine supplier Ford, reportedly for £60 million. Even after the rebadging of the team as Jaguar for the 2000 season had been announced, it was uncertain how much direct control Ford would want to take. At the pre-season launch of the Jaguar R1 car, however, Jackie Stewart announced his withdrawal to the sidelines. Paul remained in place, but the Ford suits clearly intended to run the show. Neil Ressler, a Ford vice-president, was set to take over as chairman of the Jaguar Racing team.

There was no mistaking Ford's high ambitions. They were reported to have paid some £18 million to lure Eddie Irvine into signing a three-year contract. Having narrowly failed to win the drivers' trophy for Ferrari in 1999, Irvine would be looking to carry on winning races. The outspoken Irishman suggested that relations with team-mate Johnny Herbert would be competitive: "Of course I want to beat Johnny and he wants to beat me," he said.

Ford need both drivers on the podium, as anything less than third place in the constructors' table will be viewed as a failure for Jaguar.

Team Profile

Jaguar Racing

Team Principal . . . . Neil Ressler
Chief Operating Officer . . . . Paul Stewart
Technical Director . . . . Gary Anderson

Address
Jaguar Racing Ltd, Bradbourne Drive, Tilbrook, Milton Keynes, Buckinghamshire, MK14 8BJ, UK

Internet
www.jaguar-racing.com

The Car

Chassis . . . . Jaguar R1
Engine . . . . Ford Cosworth CR-2
Power . . . . n.a.
Tyres . . . . Bridgestone

Results to end of 1999
(as Stewart)

GP Debut . . . . GP Australia 1997
GP Points 47
GP Victories 1

Johnny Herbert (car no. 8), born 27 June 1964 in Romford, Essex. F1 debut in Brazil in 1989; to end of 1999, 145 starts, 3 wins.

Eddie Irvine (car no. 7), born 10 November 1965 in Newtownards, Northern Ireland. F1 debut in Japan in 1993; to end of 1999, 97 starts, 4 wins.

Jackie Stewart announces his imminent withdrawal from the leadership of the team that he created.

Williams: Old hand springs a surprise

THE WILLIAMS TEAM LOOKED ONE of the most interesting prospects for the 2000 season, equipped with a new engine from BMW and employing one of the youngest ever F1 drivers, 20-year-old Jenson Button. Clearly, Sir Frank Williams was ready to follow a high-risk strategy in a bid to return his team to the front of the pack.

Falling short

The 1999 season had continued the poor run of form that began for the Williams team in 1998. Fifth place might not seem bad for some teams, but for an outfit that had won five constructors' championships between 1992 and 1997, it was an unacceptable falling short. One saving grace was the fine performance of Ralf Schumacher, the brother of the more famous Michael, in his first season with Williams. He was regarded by many observers as the driver of the year and his achievement was thrown into sharp relief by the woeful failure of his team-mate Alex Zanardi. It came as no suprise when Zanardi was sacked by Williams during the off season.

The announcement that a youngster was to take the driver's seat vacated by Zanardi was, by contrast, the biggest surprise of the winter in Formula One. Placed third in last year's British F3 championship, Button was obviously a driver of exceptional talent – in his karting days he had been likened to the young Ayrton Senna. But critics denounced his rapid promotion to Formula One as premature and even a potential danger to other drivers.

A star of the future

Williams technical director Patrick Head said Button was "remarkably mature" and "definitely a star of the future". In the present, though, the

young driver would need to cope not only with the demands of Formula One racing but also with a team not noted for a supportive attitude to its drivers – as Damon Hill and Heinz-Harald Frentzen would testify.

Williams knew, of course, that no drivers could hope to challenge the dominance of the McLarens and the

Ferraris without having an engine of comparable power – hence the deal struck with BMW to supply a new powerplant to replace the Supertec. For their part, BMW were tempted back into Formula One for the first time since 1987 by the desire for positive publicity to match that won by Mercedes through their McLaren

link-up. Needless to say, BMW were desperate for quick success.

However, there were rumours in the pre-season period that the BMW engine was proving unreliable in testing. Experts were unanimous that, however great its potential, the BMW-Williams combination would inevitably take time to gel.

Team Profile

Jenson Button (car no. 10), born 19 January 1980 in Frome, Somerset. F1 debut in 2000.

Ralf Schumacher (car no. 9), born 30 June 1975 in Kerpen, Germany. F1 debut in Australia in 1997; to end of 1999, 49 starts, no wins.

Team leader Sir Frank Williams, wheelchair-bound as a result of a road accident, was knighted in 1999.

Technical director Patrick Head (left) with BMW's Gerhard Berger.

BMW Williams F1

Team Principal	Sir Frank Williams
Technical Director	Patrick Head
BMW Motorsport Director	Gerhard Berger

Address
Williams Grand Prix Engineering Ltd,
Grove, Wantage, Oxon,
OX12 0DQ, UK

Internet
http://www.williamsf1.co.uk

The Car

Chassis	Williams FW22
Engine	BMW V10
Power	n.a.
Tyres	Bridgestone

Results to end of 1999

GP Debut	GP Britain 1972
GP Points	1983.5
GP Victories	103

Benetton: Dropping out of the big league

EVEN BENETTON'S KEENEST FANS have to admit that the team has lost touch with the leaders in Formula One, and is even struggling to hold a place in the middle of the pack.

Short-lived optimism

Before the start of the 1999 season Rocco Benetton, newly responsible for his family's F1 aspirations, unwisely informed the press that the worst he could imagine was a place "somewhere in the top three". There were upbeat claims about Benetton's "revolutionary" new car and an innovative braking system known as "Front Torque Transfer".

All this heady optimism quickly evaporated. At the end of a deeply disappointing season, Benetton found themselves lodged in sixth place in the constructors' table with a mere 16 points – 19 points fewer than fifth-placed Williams.

There was little optimism in the Benetton camp looking forward to the 2000 season. Although the Playlife Supertec engine had been upgraded, it was still likely to be short on power. Rocco Benetton has pinned his long-term hopes on a possible deal with Renault to supply a works engine. But this could at best be a prospect for the 2001 season.

Plenty to prove

Drivers Giancarlo Fisichella and Alexander Wurz have been retained despite last year's disappointments. Fisichella was by far the more successful of the two, finishing in the points four times, including a second place in Montreal. Wurz's best placing was fifth, in his native Austria. Both drivers clearly had plenty to prove in the course of the 2000 season.

This year's car, the B200, was unveiled in spectacular style at a Barcelona museum. Benetton hope that it will perform better than last year's model.

Team Profile

Team principal *Rocco Benetton flanked by his drivers, Alexander Wurz, left, and Giancarlo Fisichella. Wurz (car no. 11), born 15 February 1974 in Waithofen, Austria. F1 debut in Canada in 1997; to end of 1999, 35 starts, no wins. Fisichella (car no. 12), born 14 January 1973 in Rome, Italy. F1 debut in Australia in 1996; to end of 1999, 57 starts, no wins.*

Mild Seven Benetton Playlife

Team Principal	Rocco Benetton
Technical Director	Pat Symonds

Address
Benetton Formula Ltd, Whiteways Technical Centre, Enstone, Chipping Norton, Oxon, OX7 4EE, UK

Internet
www.benettonf1.com

The Car

Chassis	Benetton B200
Engine	Playlife FB 02 3.0 V10
Power	n.a.
Tyres	Bridgestone

Results to end of 1999

GP Debut	GP Brazil 1986
GP Points	821.5
GP Victories	27

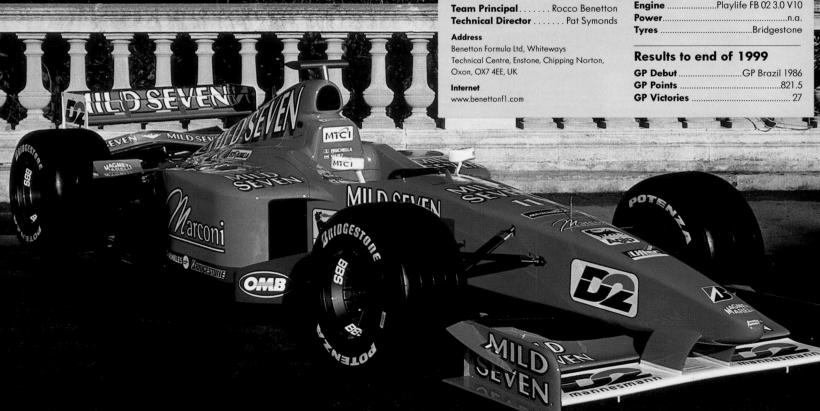

Prost: Gambling on a mix of youth and age

ALAIN PROST IS UNDERSTANDABLY impatient for a whiff of success. The second place gained by Jarno Trulli in last year's European Grand Prix at the Nürburgring was the peak of his team's achievement so far, but the rest of the season was predominantly an exercise in frustration.

With his leading driver, Trulli, tempted away to Jordan and Olivier Panis considered not to have cut the mustard, Prost has signed up a new pair for 2000: Frenchman Jean Alesi, at 35 currently the oldest driver in Formula One, and 22-year-old German Nick Heidfeld, who until the advent of Jenson Button seemed set to be this year's youngest.

Full of promise

Although only 22 at the start of this season, Heidfeld can claim a wealth of experience in Formula 3000 – he was last year's champion – and as McLaren test driver since 1998. He is widely tipped as a future star.

It is over a decade since Alesi burst on to the Formula One scene as a young driver of high promise. He has never achieved the results that his widely acknowledged brilliance seemed to merit, but his enthusiasm for the sport is undimmed.

Engine trouble

Neither driver will stand any chance of success, of course, unless the car and its engine come up to scratch. Prost reportedly threatened to end his relationship with Peugeot last season unless the manufacturer agreed to put more effort into developing a competitive engine.

The addition of English designer Alan Jenkins to the Prost team in the course of last season may strengthen their chances. Jenkins and the Prost technical supremo, John Barnard, were both key figures in the McLaren set-up that Alain Prost had behind him when he won his three world championships in his driving days. He must hope that their reunion bodes well for the season ahead.

The latest Prost car, the AP03, is expected to show the benefit of input from ex-Stewart designer Alan Jenkins.

Team Profile

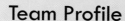

Jean Alesi (car no. 14), born 11 June 1964 in Avignon, France. F1 debut in France in 1989; to end of 1999, 167 starts, 1 win.

Nick Heidfeld (car no. 15), born 10 May 1977 in Mönchengladbach, Germany. F1 debut in 2000.

Team leader Alain Prost changed both his drivers for the 2000 season, in search of the success that had eluded him for the previous three years.

Equipe Prost-Peugeot

Team Principal .... Alain Prost
Technical Director .... John Barnard
Designer .... Alan Jenkins

Address
Equipe Prost Peugeot, Quartier des Sangliers, 7 Avenue Eugene Freyssinet, 78280 Guyancourt, France

Internet
www.prost-peugeot.com

The Car

Chassis .... Prost AP03
Engine .... Peugeot V10
Power .... 790 bhp
Tyres .... Bridgestone

Results to end of 1999

GP Debut .... GP Australia 1997
GP Points 31
GP Victories 0

Sauber: In search of the will to win

AFTER SEVEN YEARS IN FORMULA One, Sauber must feel that they have served their apprenticeship and that it is time to start making a serious impression. But instead of following an upward curve, their results have tended downwards in recent seasons. Sauber's score fell from 16 points in 1997 to 10 the following year and a mere five in 1999. Whatever story the statistics may tell, however, team boss Peter Sauber remains resolutely optimistic and committed.

The other flying Finn

Sauber's star turn in 1999 was meant to be French driver Jean Alesi, but he had a miserable time and was happy to leave at the season's end. His place is taken by Finnish driver Mika Salo, in the limelight for part of 1999 as substitute for Michael Schumacher at Ferrari. Salo would have scored his first win, at the German Grand Prix, if he had not obeyed team orders to let Eddie Irvine through. He will be keen to

establish himself as a fixture on the Formula One scene. Salo's Brazilian teammate Pedro Diniz, retained by Sauber from last year, is also hungry for success. Son of a supermarket millionaire, he is determined to

shake off the "rentadriver" tag that dogged his early career and prove that he is worth his place in Formula One on the basis of skill alone.

With its Ferrari-derived engine, the Sauber car has plenty of power.

The team also has enough financial backing from Petronas and Red Bull. But Sauber need to show that they have the professionalism and will-to-win that can pull it all together and actually get results.

Team Profile

Team leader Peter Sauber has struggled to keep a Swiss presence in Formula One since Mercedes withdrew their backing from the Sauber team in 1995.

Pedro Diniz (car no. 16), born 22 May 1970 in Sao Paulo, Brazil. F1 debut in Brazil in 1995; to end of 1999, 82 starts, no wins.

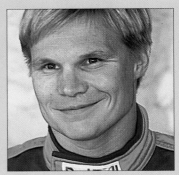

Mika Salo (car no. 17), born 30 November 1966, Helsinki, Finland. F1 debut in Japan in 1994; to end of 1999, 76 starts, no wins.

Red Bull Sauber Petronas

Team Principal ....Peter Sauber
Technical Director ....Leo Ress

Address
Team Sauber, Wildbachstrasse 9, 8340 Hinwil, Switzerland

Internet
www.sauber.ch

The Car

Chassis ....Sauber-Petronas C19
Engine ....Petronas SPE 04A
Power ....820 bhp
Tyres ....Bridgestone

Results to end of 1999

GP Debut ....GP South Africa 1993
GP Points 84
GP Victories 0

Sauber should have enough power from their Ferrari engine, rebadged as Petronas, to hold an honourable place in the middle ranks of the gird.

Arrows: Counting on better times ahead

WHEN ARROWS WERE BOUGHT BY current owner Tom Walkinshaw in 1996, they had an unenviable record as one of the least successful teams in Formula One history. Little has changed since. Despite much hype about the arrival of Nigerian Prince Malik, a new financial backer who was supposed to lift the team's profile, Arrows ended the 1999 season with only one point, scored in the first grand prix at Melbourne. Prince Malik rapidly left the scene.

Brighter prospects

For the 2000 season there is once more upbeat talk about new prospects for Arrows. A deal with Orange has reportedly provided £70 million in sponsorship. Designer Mike Coughlan has masterminded an all-new chassis, and the Arrows Hart engine has been replaced by a Renault Supertec. These developments seemed to have borne fruit when Arrows came out top in one of the pre-season testing sessions.

In 1999, an underpowered engine left Arrows vying with Minardi for places on the back two ranks of the grid. The Supertec is expected to provide more power, but it is still unlikely to be really competitive.

Reliability was the other major problem for the Arrows team in 1999. A mixture of mechanical failures and accidents meant that in the entire season drivers Pedro de la Rosa and Toranosuke Takagi could complete only nine races between them.

Going Dutch

De la Rosa, responsible for Arrows' only points placing in 1999, has been retained for 2000. But Takagi is replaced by the popular Dutch driver Jos Verstappen. Although his record in Formula One is not impressive, Verstappen is an experienced driver rated highly by many people in the motor racing world. Unfortunately, the engine and chassis are unlikely to give him much chance to compete for points.

Equipped with a new engine and a redesigned chassis, Arrows performed well in pre-season testing.

Team Profile

Arrows

Team Principal . . . . .Tom Walkinshaw
Technical Director . . . .Mike Coughlan

Address
Arrows GP International, Leafield Technical Centre, Leafield, Witney, Oxon, OX8 5PF, UK

Internet
www.arrows.com

The Car

Chassis ....Arrows A21
Engine ....Supertec FB02 V10
Power ....790 bhp
Tyres ....Bridgestone

Results to end of 1999

GP Debut..............................GP Brazil 1978
GP Points 157
GP Victories 0

Team principal Tom Walkinshaw has been in control of Arrows since 1996, but has yet to improve the team's lowly status in the sport.

Pedro de la Rosa (car no. 18), left, born 24 February 1971 in Barcelona, Spain. Made his F1 debut in Australia in 1999; to end of 1999, 16 starts, no wins.

Jos Verstappen (car no. 19), right, born 4 March 1972 in Montfort, Netherlands. Made his F1 debut in Brazil in 1994; to end of 1999, 57 starts, no wins.

13

Minardi: Minnow aims to become a big fish

MINARDI APPEAR TO BE A TEAM IN transition. Originally created by Italian car dealer and motorsport enthusiast Giancarlo Minardi, they were for many years content to be underdogs, scraping by on a minimal budget and enjoying every one of the extremely occasional points that they scored.

Money and ambition

The arrival of Gabriele Rumi of Fondmetal as dominant co-owner, however, has been a catalyst for loftier ambitions and discontent with the status of minnows. The experience of team manager Cesare Fiorio and designer Gustav Brunner, both formerly with Ferrari, has been brought in. Even more significantly, Minardi have embarked on a quest for the big-money backing that is needed for success in Formula One.

An injection of cash has come in particular from Telefonica, a Spanish telecommunications company with global ambitions. In return for Telefonica's support, Minardi has begun to take on a Spanish flavour.

For the 2000 season they have retained Spanish driver Marc Gené, with alongside him Argentinian rookie Gaston Mazzacane, apparently in response to Telefonica's desire for a driver from a Spanish-speaking country in South America.

As the 2000 season approached, Telefonica were considering the possibility of buying Minardi. If this happened, the Italian team would be moved to a new base in Spain.

Loss of independence

Although most Formula One fans regret the disappearance of small independent teams, the logic of change is, from Minardi's point of view, convincing. The single point they scored last season was their first for four years. For 2000 they have a more powerful Ford-derived engine, but no one honestly expects them to do more than make up the numbers.

Designed by Gustav Brunner, the Minardi M02 is powered by an ex-works Ford engine.

Team Profile

Team co-owner *Gabriele Rumi has adopted a more aggressive approach than the team's cheerfully ebullient founder, Giancarlo Minardi.*

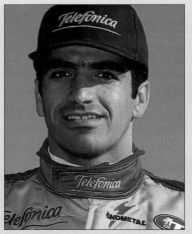

Marc Gené *(car no. 20), born 29 March 1974 in Sabadell, Spain. F1 debut in Australia in 1999; to end of 1999, 16 starts, no wins.*

Gaston Mazzacane *(car no. 21), born 8 May 1975 in La Plata, Argentina. F1 debut in 2000.*

Telefonica Minardi Fondmetal

Team Principals ....Gabriele Rumi, Giancarlo Minardi
Team Manager ....Cesare Fiorio
Technical Director..........Gustav Brunner

Address
Minardi Team SpA, Via Spallanzani 21, 48018 Faenza, Italy

Internet
www.minardi.it

The Car

Chassis...................Minardi M02
Engine ....Fondmetal V10
Power ....740 bhp
Tyres ....Bridgestone

Results to end of 1999

GP Debut ....GP Brazil 1985
GP Points 28
GP Victories 0

BAR: Recovering from a disappointing start

BRITISH AMERICAN RACING (BAR) were the most disappointing team of the 1999 season. Although it was their debut year, the team had aroused high expectations. Enthusiastic talk of a possible win in their first grand prix was given some substance by the scale of the team's financial backing, from British American Tobacco, and by the combined experience of the personnel that managing director Craig Pollock had assembled, including technical supremo Adrian Reynard, designer Malcolm Oastler, and former world champion driver Jacques Villeneuve.

Punctured expectations

Yet all the hype ended in nothing but embarassment and frustration. BAR were the only team not to score a point in the 1999 season. The hapless Villeneuve had to wait until the 12th grand prix before he finished a race.

Amazingly, in the midst of this debacle, Pollock managed to pull off a remarkable coup, inducing Honda to back the team for the 2000 season.

Looking forwards

Honda had been intending to field their own team in Formula One. It was the Japanese manufacturer's retreat from this ambition that gave Pollock the chance to make a deal. With a Honda works engine and all the manufacturer's expertise at their diposal, BAR could face the 2000 season with renewed confidence. They retained both drivers from the debut year, perhaps feeling that Jacques Villeneuve's inexperienced team-mate Ricardo Zonta had not been given any real chance to show what he could do.

Villeneuve naturally was still regarded as one of the trumps in the BAR hand – the question was not so much whether they wanted him as whether he still wanted them. In fact, the relationship between Villeneuve

Team Profile

Lucky Strike Reynard BAR Honda

Team Principal . . . . Craig Pollock
Technical Director . . . . . Adrian Reynard
Designer . . . . Malcolm Oastler

Address
British American Racing, Brackley, Northamptonshire, NN13 7BD, UK

Internet
www.britishamericanracing.com

The Car

Chassis . . . . BAR Honda 002
Engine . . . . Honda RA000E
Power . . . . 800+ bhp
Tyres . . . . Bridgestone

Results to end of 1999

GP Debut . . . . GP Australia 1999
GP Points 0
GP Victories 0

BAR are hoping that the BAR Honda 002 will prove more successful than last year's notoriously unreliable BAR 001; at least the Honda engine should give Jacques Villeneuve enough power to play with.

Jacques Villeneuve (car no. 22), born 9 April 1971 in St Jean-sur-Richelieu, Canada. F1 debut in Australia in 1996; to end of 1999, 65 starts, 11 wins.

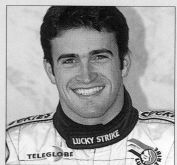

Ricardo Zonta (car no. 23), born 23 March 1976 in Curitiba, Brazil. F1 debut in Australia in 1999; to end of 1999, 12 starts, no wins.

Team leader Craig Pollock must be a man who inspires confidence, winning the backing of Honda for his team despite some dreadful results.

and Pollock, his longstanding friend and mentor, appears to have survived the strains of repeated failure, although the Canadian driver did at one point criticize Reynard for allegedly not pulling his weight.

Even in such a nightmare year as 1999 Villeneuve was able to show at moments that he is still an extremely accomplished driver, most notably in the Spanish Grand Prix, when he leapfrogged the two Ferraris at the

start to run third for 24 laps. Zonta had much more to prove and even less chance to do so, missing four races through injury. Like the entire team, he will want to put 1999 behind him and concentrate firmly on the future.

THE 2000 SEASON

The Race Diary

Australian Grand Prix • Melbourne, 12 March

Brazilian Grand Prix • São Paulo, 26 March

San Marino Grand Prix • Imola, 9 April

British Grand Prix • Silverstone, 23 April

Spanish Grand Prix • Barcelona, 7 May

European Grand Prix, Nürburgring, 21 May

Monaco Grand Prix • Monte Carlo, 4 June

Canadian Grand Prix • Montreal, 18 June

French Grand Prix • Magny-Cours, 2 July

Austrian Grand Prix • A1-Ring, 16 July

German Grand Prix • Hockenheim, 30 July

Hungarian Grand Prix • Hungaroring, 13 August

Belgian Grand Prix • Spa-Francorchamps, 27 August

Italian Grand Prix • Monza, 10 September

United States Grand Prix • Indianapolis, 24 September

Japanese Grand Prix • Suzuka, 8 October

Malaysian Grand Prix • Sepang, 22 October

12 MARCH • MELBOURNE
Australian Grand Prix

Ferrari made a triumphant start to the season as drivers Schumacher and Barrichello took maximum points while their McLaren rivals failed to finish.

Melbourne

The Circuit

The 2000 Australian Grand Prix was the fifth held at the Albert Park circuit in Melbourne. Most drivers rate it as one of their favourite courses. It is characterized by a mix of hairpins and fast corners, interspersed with a series of sweeping curves. Tyre wear can be heavy on this circuit, and it calls for maximum downforce.

Race Result

	Driver	Time
1	M. Schumacher	1:34.01.987
2	Barrichello	1:34.13.402
3	R. Schumacher	1:34.21.996
4	Villeneuve	1:34.46.434
5	Fisichella	1:34.47.152
6	Zonta	1:34.48.455

Drivers' Championship

	Driver	Points
1	M. Schumacher	10
2	Barrichello	6
3	R. Schumacher	4
4	Villeneuve	3
5	Fisichella	2
6	Zonta	1

Constructors' Championship

	Constructor	Points
1	Ferrari	16
2	BAR	4
	=Williams	4
4	Benetton	2

Track length 5.269 km (3.274 miles)
Race distance 305.602 km (189.892 miles) — 58 laps
1999 winner Eddie Irvine, Ferrari
Lap record 1:30.585 min, Heinz-Harald Frentzen, Williams-Renault, 1997

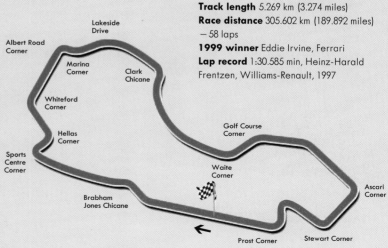

Michael Schumacher raises his fist in triumph after winning the Australian Grand Prix for the first time in his spell at Ferrari.

Fighting-fit Ferrari master McLaren

Qualification

When the qualifying session ended, the first three rows of the grid were neatly colour-coded: the silver McLarens in front, followed by the scarlet Ferraris and the yellow Jordans, a placing that reflected last season's running order.

McLaren on pole

The main contenders only emerged from their garages at the half-way mark. From then on, Hakkinen and Coulthard swapped provisional pole placings, with the battle finally going in the Finn's favour. Towards the end there was frantic activity as Michael Schumacher tried to muscle his way into the front row, but in the last minute Coulthard spun off and the yellow flags ended the session.

Tough debut

British hopeful Jenson Button had a wretched session, spending most of his time fighting with his Williams before swapping it for the spare car. With 15 minutes to go, he at last set a qualifying time, only one place ahead of fellow newcomer Gaston Mazzacane. For Jaguar, Herbert was plagued by chronic mechanical problems, but Irvine managed a creditable seventh.

Qualifying Times

1	Hakkinen	McLaren	1:30.556
2	Coulthard	McLaren	1:30.910
3	M. Schumacher	Ferrari	1:31.075
4	Barrichello	Ferrari	1:31.102
5	Frentzen	Jordan	1:31.359
6	Trulli	Jordan	1:31.504
7	Irvine	Jaguar	1:31.514
8	Villeneuve	BAR	1:31.968
9	Fisichella	Benetton	1:31.992
10	Salo	Sauber	1:32.018
11	R. Schumacher	Williams	1:32.220
12	De la Rosa	Arrows	1:32.323
13	Verstappen	Arrows	1:32.477
14	Wurz	Benetton	1:32.775
15	Heidfeld	Prost	1:33.024
16	Zonta	BAR	1:33.117
17	Alesi	Prost	1:33.197
18	Gené	Minardi	1:33.261
19	Diniz	Sauber	1:33.378
20	Herbert	Jaguar	1:33.638
21	Button	Williams	1:33.828
22	Mazzacane	Minardi	1:34.705

Michael Schumacher has never hidden his enjoyment of victory, but at Albert Park he reached new heights of elation, punching the air harder than ever before to celebrate his first victory in Australia for Ferrari. In previous years, Ferrari had always been forced to play catch-up, but for this season's first race the team hit the ground running with a car that was both fast and reliable – and Schumacher knew it.

Ferrari benefitted from other teams' shortcomings. As the first grand prix of the season, Australia tends to have a high rate of attrition, and this year was no exception with only nine out of 22 cars managing to complete the race. And the circuit was no respecter of persons, as leading teams McLaren and Jordan failed to stay the course, along with the much-vaunted Jaguar and the revamped Arrows.

Leaders drop out

At the start both McLarens made a clean getaway from the front row and their success seemed almost assured. While Hakkinen began to carve out a reasonable lead, Coulthard was easily able to hold Schumacher's Ferrari. But on lap 12, Coulthard came to a halt after a failure of the Mercedes engine's pneumatic system. Seven laps later Hakkinen's engine blew with the same problem, leaving a surprised and delighted Schumacher in the lead.

Jaguar failed miserably early on, Herbert's clutch going after a couple of laps and Irvine spinning off to avoid a collision with De la Rosa's Arrows. But Jordan seemed to be in with a chance of points for both of the drivers until their luck deserted

Schumacher basks in his triumph, alongside Ferrari manager Jean Todt.

Bright start for Villeneuve and BAR

The Melbourne Grand Prix ended with BAR, a laughing-stock last year, equal second in the championship table. The placing showed that Craig Pollock's team had immediately profited from the new reliability of their works Honda engine. Apart from Ferrari, they were the only team to get both cars across the finishing line. Netting four points more than in the whole of their barren 1999 season, BAR probably felt that they had as much to celebrate as the Scuderia.

Villeneuve led a four-car train for much of the race, showing all his defensive skills in holding up a succession of faster vehicles. He eventually took fourth place. Luck also played its part for BAR, when Mika Salo, who finished in sixth place, was disqualified for a bodywork infringement, bringing Zonta into the points.

Jacques Villeneuve with the BAR team in Melbourne.

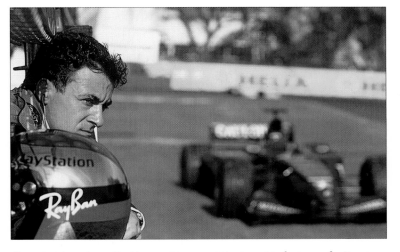

Hakkinen and Coulthard led from the start (main picture), but at the post-race news conference Hakkinen (inset) had to reflect on points lost.

them – Frentzen's gearbox gave up, while his team-mate Trulli suffered a complete hydraulic failure.

Racing Ralf

Jordan's misfortunes left the way clear for Barrichello to move up behind the leading Ferrari, and also gave Ralf Schumacher the opportunity to race to a podium finish in the new BMW-powered Williams. His youthful team-mate Jenson Button drove an equally inspiring race, fighting his way from 21st to sixth position, before his engine blew 12 laps from the end.

For a racer new to Formula One, Button drove a remarkably mature race, avoiding the myriad potential mistakes that typically take out rookie drivers on their first outing. His enthusiasm for the sport shone through in the post-race interviews. "That's the first race out of the way," he told journalists, "but now I can't wait for the next."

But the day belonged to Ferrari, whose drivers achieved a perfect score of 16 points for the team, made all the more satisfying by McLaren's zero points. An elated Schumacher said: "The first moment I got into the car, I thought, 'This is the car we are going to win the championship with,' and today proved I was right. It is not only reliable, but it is so bloody fast. It looks like being a great year for Ferrari."

French driver Jean Alesi has nothing to celebrate as his first race for Prost ends on lap 27 – although he had outlasted world champion Hakkinen.

BETWEEN THE RACES

13 March Crowds throng to Melbourne race

Despite fears that attendances at Melbourne would be down on last year, overall figures for the grand prix weekend have turned out to be almost 15,000 up on 1999. So worried were the organizers of the Australian Grand Prix that they reportedly took the step of having multi-coloured seats painted to look on television as

season, were an obvious choice. The Benetton clothing group will, however, continue to act as the F1 team's main sponsor until Renault's official re-entry into the sport in 2002.

More immediate changes include the arrival of Flavio Briatore, who will replace Rocco Benetton as team principal. The flamboyant Briatore ran the Benetton team during its glory days in the 1990s, before moving to head the engine supplier Supertec in 1997.

Williams for the 1999 season, it was believed that Montoya, who then joined the American operation, was part of a "swap" deal. It was thought likely that Williams would recall Montoya at the end of this year, but the CART driver has denied that he is under contract to the British Formula One team. The fact that newcomer Jenson Button is currently successfully occupying the spare seat at Williams only serves further to complicate the situation.

English driver Sir Sterling Moss had many successes in his driving career.

Ferrari fanatics swelled the impressive crowd for the Melbourne Grand Prix.

if they were occupied, even when empty. Relieved administrators saw 124,300 racegoers pass the turnstiles on race day. This will be an important factor in current negotiations by the circuit to extend its contract with the FIA from 2006 to 2011.

16 March Renault to take over Benetton F1 team

Last year, French motor-manufacturing giant Renault announced that it was preparing to re-enter Formula One. Today the details of this move were announced: Renault are to buy the Benetton F1 team for $120 million. For some time the ailing Benetton team has been looking for a high-profile manufacturer to supply them with a top-class engine and improve their fortunes. Renault, who so successfully partnered Benetton during the 1995

18 March Which team "owns" CART star Montoya?

The former Williams test driver Juan Montoya has found himself at the centre of controversy over his future. When former CART champion Alex Zanardi left the US Chip Ganassi team to join

21 March Ironing out the bumps in Brazil

The Interlagos circuit is traditionally one of the bumpiest in the grand prix calendar, but the course has been resurfaced this year in an effort to improve upon the unforgiving ride experienced by drivers in the past. Whether the new surface will make the track smoother remains to be seen, but tyre choice has become a matter of serious concern. Bridgestone say that they will supply the same medium and soft tyres as they did for Melbourne, but no one yet knows if the Interlagos track will be unusually abrasive or slippery.

22 March "Arise, Sir Stirling"

After being awarded a knighthood in the New Year's honours list, veteran English driver Stirling Moss has received his award at Buckingham Palace from the

Prince of Wales. The 70-year-old former grand prix star never won a world championship title, although he was a runner-up on four occasions and was considered one of the finest drivers of his era. A serious accident at Goodwood in 1962 forced him to retire from motorsport.

23 March German TV buys into Ecclestone empire

The German media conglomerate EM.TV has bought 50 per cent of Bernie Ecclestone's Formula One Administration, the company that runs the commercial side of F1. The highly complex deal is reputedly worth $1.6 billion in cash and shares. EM.TV claim that the purchase will allow them to maximize broadcasting and merchandizing rights and double television audiences from the present estimated figure of 600 million.

Ecclestone, who owns the remaining 50 per cent through a family trust, will maintain overall managerial control of Formula One Administration until a planned restructuring is completed, which should allow the company to be floated on Germany's Neuer Markt. In the near future it is possible that EM.TV will purchase a further 25 per cent of Ecclestone's company.

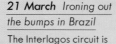

Flavio Briatore is back at Benetton, flanked by drivers Fisichella (left) and Wurz.

The promise and pitfalls of youth

FOR MOST DRIVERS THE ROUTE TO a place in Formula One is both time-consuming and arduous. A typical way to reach one of the top 22 seats in motorsport will involve early days in karting, then a path through the various junior formulas culminating in Formula 3 or Formula 3000, and finally test driving for one of the major teams. This long apprenticeship ensures that most drivers are in their early to mid twenties before they race in a grand prix. As a result, so at least the theory goes, they are fully prepared for the intense pressure and pain of Formula One.

In at the deep end

But what about those drivers who are given an F1 drive while relative youngsters? The British media frenzy that followed the news that 20-year-old Jenson Button would race alongside Ralf Schumacher for Williams also provoked a debate about whether he was too young for the job.

Jenson Button, aged 20, shows his confidence in front of the media.

Emerson Fittipaldi won the world championship in 1974 at 25 – the age at which many drivers start their F1 careers.

Expert media commentators and current and former drivers were canvassed for their opinions. Jackie Stewart and Mika Hakkinen adopted a negative tone, believing that Button did not have the experience to flourish in a famously tough team like Williams, while a more sizeable bevy of pundits, from Sterling Moss to Michael Schumacher, accentuated the positive side.

Alain Prost, who had employed Button as a test driver before releasing him to Williams, delivered

this assessment: "He is mature for his age and he is quick... I think he is something special."

While Button is the youngest British driver to race in Formula One, he is by no means the youngest F1 driver overall. That crown belongs to 19-year-old New Zealander Mike Thackwell, who was given a race at Montreal in 1980 (the year of Button's birth). Chris Amon – another New Zealander – was also aged 19 at

his first GP in 1963. Amon gained five poles in 96 races, although he acquired a slightly dubious accolade as the best driver never to win a championship grand prix.

Other young drivers thrown in at the deep end of Formula One have included Peter Collins (20 at the 1952 Swiss GP) and, more recently, Rubens Barrichello (20 at the 1993 South African GP). The most successful of all the youth brigade is Emerson Fittipaldi, who won the 1972 world championship in his third season aged just 25.

Talent and temperament

On balance it would seem that age is not a defining factor in the overall equation of racing success. More important are raw talent, the ability to handle pressure, a good quality machine to drive, and the full support of a good team.

Button certainly has plenty of time to make his mark, when you consider the ages of some former Williams world champions: Alan Jones (33), Alain Prost (37), and, granddaddy of them all, Nigel Mansell (39). Perhaps we will be lauding Button's success in 2019.

Chris Amon, the second youngest man ever to drive in a Formula One race, enjoyed a successful career in the 1960s.

26 MARCH • SAO PAULO
Brazilian Grand Prix

In a **repeat** of Melbourne, the two **McLarens** occupied the **front of the grid** but ended up **pointless**, as a **dominant** Michael Schumacher **cruised to victory.**

São Paulo

Race Result

	Driver	Time
1	M. Schumacher	1:31.35.271
2	Fisichella	1:32.15.169
3	Frentzen	1:32.17.539
4	Trulli	1:32.48.051
5	R. Schumacher	1 lap behind
6	Button	1 lap behind

Coulthard was disqualified after finishing in second place.

Drivers' Championship

	Driver	Points
1	M. Schumacher	20
2	Fisichella	8
3	Barrichello	6
	=R. Schumacher	6
5	Frentzen	4
6	Trulli	3
	=Villeneuve	3
8	Button	1
	=Zonta	1

Constructors' Championship

	Constructor	Points
1	Ferrari	26
2	Benetton	8
3	Jordan	7
	=Williams	7
5	BAR	4

The Circuit

The Interlagos circuit, officially called the Autodromo José Carlos, is situated on the southern outskirts of São Paulo. Despite resurfacing work carried out since last season, the track remains bumpy. The uneven surface and the mix of slow and fast curves tests both cars and drivers.

Track length 4.311 km (2.679 miles)
Race distance 306.081 km (190.209 miles) — 71 laps
1999 winner Mika Hakkinen, McLaren-Mercedes
Lap record 1:14.755 min, Michael Schumacher, Ferrari, 2000

Bico de Pato

Mergulho

Ferradura   Pinheirinho

Junção

"S" do Senna

Curva do Sol

Descida do Lago

Reta Oposta

Ferrari celebrate another victory for Schumacher.

Schumacher stretches the lead

Qualification

After the event, Mika Hakkinen described qualifying at Interlagos as "complicated" — not a bad description of a session plagued not only by rain but by collapsing advertising hoardings!

The McLarens and Ferraris came out early in the session as clouds threatened a downpour. Many of the drivers were just working up to their flying laps, however, when the hoardings began to fall — the last of them landing on Alesi's Prost. The red flag was brought out three times. As soon as these interruptions were over the rain began, and the session was effectively over.

Order out of chaos

The chaotic proceedings had no effect on the familiar order of the front four: Hakkinen, Coulthard, Schumacher, and Barrichello. Behind them, less than a second separated Fisichella in the fifth spot from Alesi in 15th. Irvine qualified sixth for Jaguar, although, as he pointed out, if he had been a tenth of a second slower he might have ended up "looking a complete idiot".

At the back of the grid, Sauber had a problem with collapsing rear wings. Despite qualifying, they withdrew from the grand prix.

Qualifying Times

1	Hakkinen	McLaren	1:14.111
2	Coulthard	McLaren	1:14.285
3	M. Schumacher	Ferrari	1:14.508
4	Barrichello	Ferrari	1:14.636
5	Fisichella	Benetton	1:15.375
6	Irvine	Jaguar	1:15.425
7	Frentzen	Jordan	1:15.455
8	Zonta	BAR	1:15.484
9	Button	Williams	1:15.490
10	Villeneuve	BAR	1:15.515
11	R. Schumacher	Williams	1:15.561
12	Trulli	Jordan	1:15.627
13	Wurz	Benetton	1:15.664
14	Verstappen	Arrows	1:15.704
15	Alesi	Prost	1:15.715
16	De la Rosa	Arrows	1:16.002
17	Herbert	Jaguar	1:16.250
18	Gené	Minardi	1:16.380
19	Heidfeld	Prost	1:17.112
20	Diniz	Sauber	1:17.178
21	Mazzacane	Minardi	1:17.512
22	Salo	Sauber	1:18.703

Opting for a two-stop strategy, the Ferraris were carrying a much lighter fuel load at the start of the race than the one-stop McLarens. They gambled on exploiting the weight difference to establish an early lead — and the gamble paid off. Michael Schumacher stayed on maximum points for the season while, to compound McLaren's misery, Coulthard was disqualified after finishing second.

Starting on the second row behind the McLarens, the Ferraris surprised everyone with their early pace and aggression. Schumacher jumped Coulthard as the cars pulled away from the grid and, a lap later, he powered past Hakkinen as well, an experience the German later described as "quite entertaining". Meanwhile Barrichello also passed David Coulthard.

Whether the two-stop strategy would have given Schumacher victory in a straight fight with Hakkinen was never settled because the Finn was once more let down by his engine. He retired on lap 31, leaving Schumacher comfortably in command.

By then Barrichello's race had also ended, through hydraulic trouble, and Coulthard was left to chase Schumacher. The Scottish driver did exceptionally well, given that he had problems with his gears virtually throughout the race. As Schumacher also encountered mechanical trouble, in the end both leaders concentrated on nursing their ailing cars home.

Further down the field there was enough overtaking momentarily to silence F1's vocal critics. Arrows' Jos Verstappen cut through the field from 14th on the grid to third place by lap 31, before fading, and Jordan's Jarno Trulli finished fifth from 12th on the grid. Fisichella drove impressively to give Benetton a podium place, and Williams had another good day. There was more misery for Jaguar, however, both drivers again failing to complete.

Technical knock-out

The post-race inspection revealed that Coulthard's car infringed technical regulations. He was stripped of his hard-earned six points and everyone else moved up a place. In this rather unsatisfactory way Button, lifted from seventh to sixth, became the youngest driver ever to win a point in Formula One.

For the last six seasons, the winner in Brazil has won the championship. Schumacher commented ironically that if this was true, he could "go home now and watch the rest of the season on television". The McLaren team no doubt wished that he would!

Right: Coulthard put in a doughty performance but got nothing for it. Below: One lap into the race and Schumacher powers past Hakkinen on the inside.

Frentzen returned to last season's form with a solid points finish for Jordan.

Young Jenson Button, seen here with BMW motorsport director Gerhard Berger, benefitted from Coulthard's disqualification to take sixth place, confirming a better-than-expected start to his F1 career.

BETWEEN THE RACES

30 March *Michelin to provide rubber for Jaguar in 2001*

As part of their re-entry into Formula One, French manufacturer Michelin have announced a deal to supply Jaguar with tyres for the 2001 season. Michelin racing director Pierre Dupasquier outlined company policy: "We have already started our tyre test programme at our research centre in France and are looking forward to meeting the challenge of Formula One." Jaguar have now joined Williams in changing over to Michelin, but it remains to be seen how many other teams will break from their allegiance to Bridgestone.

4 April *Coulthard appeal rejected*

Following today's hearing by the FIA's International Court of Appeal in Paris, the decision by race stewards in Brazil to disqualify David Coulthard has been upheld. After crossing the line in second place at Interlagos, Coulthard was disqualified by race scrutineers who judged that the Scottish driver's car exceeded, by two millimetres, the tolerances

The collar-shaped harness that all F1 drivers will be wearing next season.

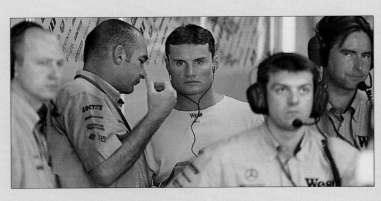

The moment when David Coulthard, centre, heard the news of his disqualification.

permitted at the rear edges of the front wing. Immediately after disqualification the McLaren team appealed against the ruling, claiming that the bodywork change was a natural consequence of bottoming and heavy vibration caused by the Sao Paulo track. The FIA decision means that McLaren have yet to score any points this season.

4 April *Villeneuve rumoured to be searching for a new seat*

Although Jacques Villeneuve has said that he would like to stay with BAR, he has made it clear that if the team does not begin to get results soon he will look elsewhere for a ride in 2001. Feelers have been put out to McLaren, and it is believed that Jaguar would be keen to sign the former world champion. As the

second highest paid driver in Formula One, Villeneuve would be an expensive option. But he might be persuaded to moderate his financial demands in return for a serious chance to win races.

6 April *Prost look on the bright side*

Despite their poor start to the season, Prost technical director Alan Jenkins remains upbeat and believes that the team has managed to sort out most of the problems that have produced just one finish so far this year. Following extensive testing at Silverstone and in Barcelona, the Guyancourt team have adjusted the car's rear and front wings and made improvements to the engine. "We will also arrive at Imola," said Jenkins, "with many modifications to the electrical installations and to the electronics of the car, which should enable us to make better use of the free practice sessions and be more reliable in Sunday's race."

Alain Prost manages a wry smile in spite of the problems his team are facing.

7 April *Fine for Brazilians*

The World Motor Sport Council fined the organizers of the Brazilian Grand Prix $100,000 for allowing advertising hoardings to fall on the track during qualifying. The incident caused three disruptions to the session and an accident to Jean Alesi's Prost. The Brazilians will be relieved that they have been allowed to retain the right to hold the grand prix next season.

8 April *Safety first with HANS*

A new safety system designed to protect the driver during high-speed crashes has been introduced by the FIA. The Head and Neck Support (HANS) system has been developed over three years and is designed to minimize the neck injuries encountered in Formula One. The device consists of a collar-shaped harness that fits over the shoulders and is attached to the helmet and seat belts. FIA President Max Mosley said that all the teams would be given the system to use during testing for the rest of the season, and that if there were no unforeseen problems HANS would become mandatory in 2001.

The HANS system was chosen in preference to airbags, as airbag sensors were unable to differentiate between an actual crash and high-speed braking or the hitting of kerbs.

To pit or not to pit, that is the question

SINCE REFUELLING BECAME compulsory, at the start of the 1994 season, pit-stops have taken on a new importance in Formula One. Before 1994, tyre wear was the main factor in bringing a car into the pits, and the nature of the circuit determined how many stops would be made in a race. Consequently, a good pit-stop was merely a quick one, with the best pit crews being able to replace tyres in around five seconds.

One stop or two?

Since 1994, pit-stops have become much more complex. The teams have to compute their own fuel loads (and likely tyre wear) against those of their rivals, weighing up the advantages and disadvantages of a one-stop or two-stop strategy. This season's Brazilian Grand Prix provided good examples of both these strategies. The Ferrari team reasoned that if Michael Schumacher, on the second row of the grid, was to overtake the McLarens he would need a considerably lighter fuel load, and that once past Coulthard and Hakkinen he would be able to build up a sufficient lead to pit twice and still stay in front. Further down the order, Benetton adopted a one-stop

Ross Brawn of Ferrari is the acknowledged master of racing strategy.

strategy, with Fisichella running a heavy fuel load from the start. This initially cost him several places but towards the end of the race allowed him to pass middle-order rivals, who stopped twice, for a podium finish.

Sense of timing

Being able to think on your feet is also an important requirement for a team manager. Ross Brawn, now with Ferrari, was one of the first to grasp the importance of the exact timing of

a pit-stop – the need to be constantly aware of slower cars on the circuit, and, if possible, make sure the driver comes out of the pits with clear track ahead of him and not behind a gaggle of back markers fighting each other for position. By such decisions races are often won or lost.

The biggest single factor that can undermine the best-laid strategies is bad weather, which in F1 terms means heavy rain alternating with dry periods. When rain starts to fall,

team chiefs face the dilemma of whether to bring the driver in for wet tyres or leave him out in the hope that it will only be a quick shower. The worst scenario is if persistent rain starts to fall just after a driver has made a stop. He then has to be called in again for a tyre change, losing invaluable seconds.

Keeping a weather eye

Most teams resign themselves to the fact that intermittent heavy rain will make pit-stop strategies something of a lottery. But in last season's French Grand Prix, Jordan turned bad weather to their advantage. They stationed a team member with a mobile phone a few miles upwind of the circuit, and he relayed news of an impending monsoon-like rainstorm. Reckoning that such heavy rain would bring out the safety car for a long period, the team modified Frentzen's two-stop strategy to a single stop, calculating that he had just enough fuel to drive to the finish. This gamble paid off handsomely, with Frentzen taking the chequered flag.

The Arrows crew are on their marks as one of their drivers is called in.

9 APRIL • IMOLA
San Marino Grand Prix

The Circuit

The Autodromo Enzo and Dino Ferrari at Imola has undergone extreme change since 1994, the year when Ayrton Senna and Roland Ratzenberger were killed on the circuit. Chicanes have tamed the Tamburello and Villeneuve curves, while the Variante Bassa corner has been made less extreme. The circuit still puts a very heavy strain on transmission, brakes, and tyres.

Track length 4.929 km (3.063 miles)
Race distance 305.598 km (189.895 miles) — 62 laps
1999 winner Michael Schumacher, Ferrari
Lap record 1:25.531 min, Heinz-Harald Frentzen, Williams-Renault, 1997

Race Result

	Driver	Time
1	M. Schumacher	1:31.39.776
2	Hakkinen	1:31.40.944
3	Coulthard	1:32.30.784
4	Barrichello	1:33.09.052
5	Villeneuve	1 lap behind
6	Salo	1 lap behind

Drivers' Championship

	Driver	Points
1	M. Schumacher	30
2	Barrichello	9
3	Fisichella	8
4	Hakkinen	6
	=R. Schumacher	6
6	Villeneuve	5
7	Frentzen	4
	=Coulthard	4
9	Trulli	3

Button, Salo, Zonta, 1 point.

Constructors' Championship

	Constructor	Points
1	Ferrari	39
2	McLaren	10
3	Benetton	8
4	Jordan	7
	=Williams	7
6	BAR	6
7	Sauber	1

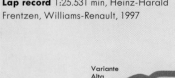

Tosa
Piratella
Villeneuve
Acque Minerali
Variante Alta
Tamburello
Rivazza
Variante Bassa

Michael Schumacher on the way to a repeat of last year's victory on Ferrari's home circuit.

Their first **podium places** of the **season** brought **little joy** to McLaren as the apparently **unstoppable** Michael **Schumacher** recorded his **third win** in a row.

Hakkinen is mugged by his German stalker

Qualification

The long-running duel between McLaren and Ferrari resumed at Imola. Ferrari at one point thought that they had done enough to get their man on pole in front of a home crowd, but in the end Schumacher had to give way to Hakkinen — one of the great qualifiers of Formula One.

Hakkinen said afterwards that it had been the toughest qualifying session in the season so far, and that he was especially pleased to be at the front given the difficulty of overtaking on the Imola circuit. The way seemed open for Hakkinen to chip away at Schumacher's lead in the drivers' championship.

Benetton off colour

Coulthard and Barrichello occupied the second row, with the Williams of Ralf Schumacher and Frentzen's Jordan directly behind them. Surprisingly, Giancarlo Fisichella had a terrible session. At Interlagos he had been up with McLaren and Ferrari, and it had seemed that Benetton might be about to turn a corner. At Imola, however, he found himself back in 19th position, deep among the no-hopers. It was embarrassing for Benetton, and humiliating for Fisichella.

Qualifying Times

1	Hakkinen	McLaren	1:24.714
2	M. Schumacher	Ferrari	1:24.805
3	Coulthard	McLaren	1:25.014
4	Barrichello	Ferrari	1:25.242
5	R.Schumacher	Williams	1:25.871
6	Frentzen	Jordan	1:25.892
7	Irvine	Jaguar	1:25.929
8	Trulli	Jordan	1:26.002
9	Villeneuve	BAR	1:26.124
10	Diniz	Sauber	1:26.238
11	Wurz	Benetton	1:26.281
12	Salo	Sauber	1:26.336
13	De la Rosa	Arrows	1:26.349
14	Zonta	BAR	1:26.814
15	Alesi	Prost	1:26.824
16	Verstappen	Arrows	1:26.845
17	Herbert	Jaguar	1:27.051
18	Button	Williams	1:27.135
19	Fisichella	Benetton	1:27.253
20	Mazzacane	Minardi	1:28.161
21	Gené	Minardi	1:28.333
22	Heidfeld	Prost	1:28.361

In front of thousands of deliriously cheering Ferrari *tifosi*, Michael Schumacher pursued and finally overcame Mika Hakkinen to make it three wins out of three. Schumacher's brilliant start to the season left his main rivals fighting over the crumbs from a banquet that had taken the German driver 24 points clear of the reigning champion.

Overtaking in Formula One is never easy but at some circuits — of which Imola is one — it is nearly impossible. David Coulthard estimated that a driver would need a five-second lap advantage to pass a rival, which in effect meant overtaking back markers only. On race day, the only route up the ladder would come through quick pit-stops or a blistering start.

The race began well for McLaren as Schumacher's wheel-spinning Ferrari allowed Hakkinen to get away cleanly into the lead. Schumacher admitted it was one of the worst starts of his career, but it did not stop him ruthlessly chopping across Coulthard, who would otherwise have followed his team-mate into the distance. Coulthard was forced to slow to avoid hitting Schumacher, which in turn allowed Barrichello to get ahead of the Scot — and slow him up for much of the remainder of the race.

The other driver to benefit from a good start was Jacques Villeneuve. The BAR driver shot from ninth to fifth by the time he reached the first corner. Of his getaway, Villeneuve said: "It was one of the best of my career, if not *the* best. I don't think I could ever do a start like that again." As had been the case in Australia, the speed of the BAR was not up to that of its pursuers, and Villeneuve spent the rest of the race fighting off a gaggle of drivers including Trulli, Irvine, Ralf Schumacher, and Mika Salo.

Out in front

With the start over, the grand prix settled down to a steady rhythm, waiting for pit-stops to produce any positional changes. The two front men, Hakkinen and Schumacher, drove superb races, carving out a

Coulthard tracks Barrichello around the circuit — a pursuit that lasted 46 laps until the Scotsman finally passed the Brazilian in the pits.

The McLaren drivers find it hard to endure another Schumacher celebration.

Jaguar driver Herbert again saw the leaders disappear into the distance.

Villeneuve showed his concentration to hold fifth place after a flying start.

substantial lead over the rest of the pack. When they both pitted for their first stop on lap 27, Hakkinen safely held on to his early advantage.

Schuey takes over

On lap 43 Hakkinen suddenly lost power as an electronic gremlin caused his engine to cut out momentarily. This allowed Schumacher to close on the Finn. When Hakkinen came in for his second stop on the next lap, the Ferrari driver put down the hammer

with a clear road ahead. Schumacher pitted on lap 48 and was able to rejoin the track a good three seconds clear of Hakkinen. With that the race for first place was effectively over.

The second round of pit-stops did, however, go McLaren's way when Barrichello and Coulthard came in. The Scot was able to leapfrog the slower-moving Barrichello, who was driving with a broken seat harness. But two podium places were small consolation for the McLaren team.

12 April *Verstappen takes up new sport*

After admitting that the Brazilian Grand Prix had proved too physically demanding for him, Arrows driver Jos Verstappen revealed that he has changed his exercise regime to better prepare himself for the rigours of Formula One. Instead of increasing time in the gym, Verstappen took the unusual step of training with Gloucester Rugby Club. Arrows chairman Tom Walkinshaw, a self-confessed rugby fanatic and owner of the Gloucester club, provided facilities for Verstappen to improve his endurance fitness.

Jos Verstappen has had problems meeting the physical demands of F1.

13 April *Name the F1 cheats, says Bernie Ecclestone*

In the light of recent speculation over teams cheating during last season, Bernie Ecclestone has called upon the FIA to name those responsible. "At the moment a cloud of suspicion is hanging over everyone," said Ecclestone, "and the finger is being pointed all over the place. It is affecting everyone, which is not fair."

The FIA believes that at least one team used sensors intended for limiting speed in the pit lane to, in effect, provide a form of traction-control, which is banned in Formula One. Speaking for the FIA, Max Mosley said that he did not have sufficient evidence to launch a prosecution. "I am not going to name the team," Mosley insisted, "but they were prepared to do something that was not a question of interpreting the rules but was quite clearly outside them. We don't have 100 per cent proof, but we are sure enough to know this is something we have got to put a stop to." Mosley did say, however, that the team had not been a championship contender, and that no such traction-control system had been used by anyone during this season. [See feature opposite]

14 April *McNish signing shows Toyota are serious about F1*

Toyota have announced that Scottish driver Allan McNish has been signed up as their F1 test and development driver.

Alan McNish won at Le Mans in 1998.

Donnington Park is in the running as a possible venue for the British Grand Prix.

McNish, a winner of the Le Mans 24-hour race in 1998, already has an association with Toyota and will use the Toyota GT-One car to collect data on circuits, tyres, and hydraulic systems performance in preparation for the company's move into Formula One, which is scheduled to occur by 2002 at the latest. Ove Andersson, president of the Cologne-based Toyota Motorsport, welcomed McNish's arrival: "His speed, consistency, and technical knowledge are now invaluable skills to us as we continue development towards our entry into Formula One."

14 April *Paul Stewart steps down from his post at Jaguar*

In another blow for the troubled Jaguar team, Jackie Stewart has announced that his son Paul is stepping down from his position as chief operating officer, after being diagnosed as suffering from cancer of the colon. Paul Stewart has entered the Mayo Clinic in the United States where he will undergo a course of chemotherapy. He is expected eventually to make a full recovery.

15 April *Donnington a contender in race to hold British Grand Prix*

The battle between Silverstone and Brands Hatch to hold the rights to stage the British Grand Prix in 2002 took a new turn when it emerged that Donnington Park might be a possible venue. The management of Brands Hatch have approached Donnington, which last staged an F1 grand prix in 1993, to see whether it could act as a back-up circuit if planning permission to hold the race at Brands was rejected by Kent County Council. Although Donnington is well below the standards laid down for Formula One, it might prove cheaper to upgrade the circuit there than carry out the $55 million alterations called for at Brands Hatch, which is also the subject of vociferous local protests over the felling of trees and change of land use.

Ban on Black Box "cheating"

19 April *Panis rejected offers of F1 seat*

French driver Olivier Panis revealed that he turned down offers to drive with Arrows and Williams for the 2000 season. The former Prost driver explained that he preferred to accept the role of McLaren test driver to "find out what a big team was all about and to work with the top engineers".

Olivier Panis would rather test-drive for McLaren than race for other teams.

Although Panis was tempted by the idea of driving for Williams, he was only offered a short-term contract which he thought would not improve his chances of a top F1 ride in 2001.

22 April *The heavens open over Silverstone*

So heavy was the rain at Silverstone at the start of the race weekend that police turned away thousands of fans who had hoped to attend qualifying. Car paddocks intended to hold 35,000 vehicles turned into quagmires, and to avoid potential mayhem on the race day itself the organizers took the drastic step of restricting access on the Saturday. The decision has caused uproar among British Formula One enthusiasts, and has embarrassingly highlighted the shortcomings of the facilities at Silverstone.

Heavy rain at Silverstone made practice trying for spectators and drivers alike.

F1 CARS ARE FITTED WITH AN Electronic Engine Management System, or Black Box – a complex piece of electronics that not only sends readings of the car's performance to the pits but also controls the basic mechanical workings of the car, including the engine, gearbox, clutch, acceleration, brakes, and suspension.

Bending the rules

After analyzing last season's car telemetry, the FIA concluded that at least one team had been using their Black Box software to circumvent rules banning the use of traction-control devices. Apparently, electronic

The rear light shines in the pit lane, showing that the pit-lane limiter is on.

pit-lane limiters, designed to ensure that cars keep within the speed limits when entering and leaving the pits, were being used to limit wheel spin at the start, and possibly at other times.

FIA clampdown

Determined to stop what they saw as "cheating", the FIA put in place new procedures to monitor the teams more closely, and proposed a total ban on electronic pit-lane limiters.

Although some drivers, including Benetton's Alexander Wurz, welcomed the prospect of regulating their speed in the pits manually, others were concerned that this might prove dangerous. Michael Schumacher commented: "If you are going down the pits watching your speed dial you

will not be able to look out for other cars coming out of their pit."

Faced with a barrage of criticism from the teams, the FIA suggested a compromise. It was agreed that the sensors that judged pit-lane speeds would be moved from the rear (drive) wheels to the front wheels, so they could not be used as an aid at the start.

No hiding place

In addition, to avoid the clandestine use of pit-lane limiters, the car's low-visibility rear light would flash and the fuel flap remain open whenever the limiter was switched on.

The new system came into force at the British Grand Prix. The teams and drivers generally welcomed the change, and it seems likely to stay.

23 APRIL • SILVERSTONE
British Grand Prix

David Coulthard established his claim to be **taken seriously** as a drivers' **championship contender** with an **exhilarating victory** in his home grand prix.

Race Result

	Driver	Time
1	Coulthard	1:28.50.108
2	Hakkinen	1:28.51.585
3	M. Schumacher	1:29.10.025
4	R. Schumacher	1:29.31.420
5	Button	1:29.47.867
6	Trulli	1:30.09.381

Drivers' Championship

	Driver	Points
1	M. Schumacher	34
2	Coulthard	14
3	Hakkinen	12
4	Barrichello	9
=	R. Schumacher	9
6	Fisichella	8
7	Villeneuve	5
8	Frentzen	4
=	Trulli	4

Button, 3 points. Salo, Zonta, 1 point.

Constructors' Championship

	Constructor	Points
1	Ferrari	43
2	McLaren	26
3	Williams	12
4	Benetton	8
=	Jordan	8
6	BAR	6
7	Sauber	1

The Circuit

The future of Silverstone as the home of the British Grand Prix may be in doubt, but it currently remains one of the most exciting Formula One circuits. Chicanes have been constructed on many bends, but the fast corners always promise spectacular racing.

Track length 5.142 km (3.194 miles)
Race distance 308.52 km (191.64 miles) – 60 laps
1999 winner David Coulthard, McLaren
Lap record 1:24.475 min, Michael Schumacher, Ferrari, 1997

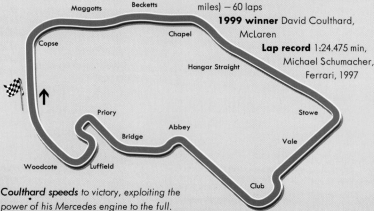

Coulthard speeds to victory, exploiting the power of his Mercedes engine to the full.

McLaren are back in business as Ferrari falter

Qualification

A rain-spoiled practice session on Friday meant that the teams entered qualifying with little idea how they might perform.

Despite the fact that Silverstone was half-empty – as a result of restrictions on access imposed to protect rain-affected parking areas – the excitement on the circuit was electric. Conditions improved by the minute as the track dried, so each new lap tended to be faster than the one before it.

Brazilian on pole

Of the top drivers, Barrichello laid down the marker after five minutes with a tentative 1:32.639. He was followed by nine others all setting best times until the Brazilian finally reclaimed pole position in the final seconds with a blistering 1: 25.703.

Second place for Frentzen hinted that Jordan had regained some of last season's speed. But British fans were most delighted with the performance of Williams, as local hero Button took a place on the third row of the grid, ahead of team-mate Ralf Schumacher. It was a frustrating session for Irvine and Villeneuve, each of whom was fastest quite late on, but ended up with a modest placing.

Qualifying Times

1	Barrichello	Ferrari	1:25.703
2	Frentzen	Jordan	1:25.706
3	Hakkinen	McLaren	1:25.741
4	Coulthard	McLaren	1:26.088
5	M. Schumacher	Ferrari	1:26.161
6	Button	Williams	1:26.733
7	R. Schumacher	Williams	1:26.786
8	Verstappen	Arrows	1:26.793
9	Irvine	Jaguar	1:26.818
10	Villeneuve	BAR	1:27.025
11	Trulli	Jordan	1:27.164
12	Fisichella	Benetton	1:27.253
13	Diniz	Sauber	1:27.301
14	Herbert	Jaguar	1:27.461
15	Alesi	Prost	1:27.559
16	Zonta	BAR	1:27.772
17	Heidfeld	Prost	1:27.806
18	Salo	Sauber	1:28.110
19	De la Rosa	Arrows	1:28.135
20	Wurz	Benetton	1:28.205
21	Gené	Minardi	1:28.253
22	Mazzacane	Minardi	1:29.174

Amidst the rain and mud that plagued Silverstone, a ray of sunshine beamed down on McLaren and, especially, David Coulthard. Ferrari's early-season domination was brought to a halt as the Scottish driver won his second British Grand Prix in a row. Last season DC had been somewhat lucky, profiting from the misfortunes of others, but this year he drove a superb race that vaulted him into second place in the drivers' table and established him as a genuine contender for the championship.

Left: Coulthard revelled in the experience of winning at Silverstone for the second consecutive season.

Below: Ralf Schumacher and Button picked up points for Williams.

Psychologically, the defining moment of the British Grand Prix occurred on lap 31. David Coulthard was pursuing Rubens Barrichello, who had held the lead since making a good getaway from pole at the start. A minor error by the Ferrari driver through the Becketts S-bend gave Coulthard his chance. In an overtaking manoeuvre reminiscent of Nigel Mansell's on Nelson Piquet in the 1987 British Grand Prix, Coulthard tore down the Hangar straight to sweep past Barrichello as they came out of Stowe corner. "I found myself thinking of the move Nigel pulled on Nelson Piquet," said Coulthard, "and I thought, 'Right, let's give it a go'."

Stamp of authority

The crowd roared their approval as the McLaren driver took first place, and even though he temporarily lost the lead a few laps later after going in for his sole pit-stop, Coulthard had unmistakably stamped his authority on the race. Barrichello soon ran out of luck altogether – his hydraulics failed, forcing him out of the contest.

Schuey muscles in

It seemed that this incident would signal a fruitless afternoon for Ferrari, as Michael Schumacher had made a poor start, which saw him pushed back into eighth place by Villeneuve, brother Ralf, and Jenson Button. Schumacher, however, fought his way back with some typically muscular driving and, with the help of attrition to the front runners, eventually won himself a podium finish.

Like Ferrari, Jordan experienced a mixed day's fortunes. Heinz-Harald Frentzen seemed ready to capitalize on his front-row grid position, and even if his two-stop pit strategy was arguably less sound than that adopted by single-stoppers McLaren and Ferrari, he looked good until a failing gearbox ended his race. Trulli did better, however, earning a single point after slipping past Villeneuve. Both Williams cars stopped twice, with Button having to give way to team-mate Ralf Schumacher in a race that did both drivers much credit.

Jaguar's misery continued, made worse by the fact that the British Grand Prix was supposed to act as a showcase for the improved Jaguar car. As it turned out, Silverstone was not to be painted green – Herbert and Irvine limped over the line in 12th and 13th places respectively. The only consolation for the Jaguar team was that both cars made it to the finish.

Keeping in touch

Hakkinen lost out to Coulthard at the start, and seemed unhappy with the balance of his car. But he persevered, and towards the end of the race picked up speed to take the fastest lap and press Coulthard to the line. The 16 points were exactly what McLaren needed if they were to stay in touch with Ferrari and Schumacher.

Jordan are left holding the baby

Eddie Jordan has a baby buggy fitted out for Frentzen to drive.

Heinz-Harald Frentzen and the Jordan team were in high spirits at Silverstone, celebrating the arrival of Frentzen's baby daughter Lea. But the failure of the German driver to finish after taking a place at the front of the grid was typical of a disappointing season so far. Poor reliability has undermined his best efforts. Third in the drivers' title race last year, this season he has had only one finish in four starts.

Coulthard

24 April *Silverstone — the recriminations begin*

The British media have joined Bernie Ecclestone and frustrated fans in condemning the organization of the rain-soaked British Grand Prix. Many F1 enthusiasts had been prevented by the authorities from attending qualifying, and on race day many more failed to get to the circuit because of five-hour traffic jams.

Although the Silverstone management promised to reimburse both fans unable to attend qualifying and those who missed the race, *The Times* thundered: "For spectators who had paid hundreds of pounds, it was the pits. Incompetent management, inept scheduling and all-too predictable April weather denied them the chance to cheer on their heroes." Ecclestone criticized the organizers for not taking the weather into account, but was himself attacked for having brought back the grand prix's traditional July date to Easter.

24 April *Williams lukewarm over Button*

Despite gaining two championship points in his first British Grand Prix, Jenson Button has been criticized by team boss Sir Frank Williams. "He finished fifth, but maybe it could have been fourth or third," said Williams. "There's been much more hype this weekend than previously. It was a concern, and although he handled it very well it does cost him focus." Williams's remarks come at a time when Button's personal management team is trying to raise his public profile in the hope of securing a definite ride for 2001.

27 April *BAR to sue Mika Salo*

Sauber driver Mika Salo has found himself facing the unwelcome attentions of former employer British American Racing. Salo replaced the injured Ricardo Zonta at BAR for

Mike Gascoyne, a key player in the Jordan team, is poached by Benetton.

three races during the early part of the 1999 season, and BAR claim that the Finnish driver broke an exclusivity contract when he signed to Ferrari later in the season (following the injury to Michael Schumacher). BAR have threatened to sue Salo and his management company Sporting Elite, unless they are paid substantial damages which are thought to run to several hundred thousand dollars.

The strangest part of BAR's claim against Salo is that he might have shared technical secrets with Ferrari. Given that BAR failed to win a single point last season, cynics might wonder just exactly what those secrets were, and did they play a part in securing the World Constructors' Championship for Ferrari?

28 April *Gascoyne to leave Jordan for Benetton*

Benetton have announced that Jordan technical director Mike Gascoyne will join the team on a five-year contract from July 2001. Gascoyne is highly rated in the F1 world and is believed to have played a major role in Jordan's rise to prominence over the last couple of years. The new Benetton managing director, Flavio Briatore, told journalists: "They have given me the task to build a team that can win the world championship. We have a good team here but I need to add the best of the best to make it strong. Mike falls into this category."

1 May *Hakkinen says team orders are inevitable*

World champion Mika Hakkinen has told a German newspaper that McLaren will have to apply team orders at some point in the season. Hakkinen failed to say to whom the team orders would be applied, although his assumption must be that he would be the Number One driver.

2 May *Coulthard crash disaster*

A private jet carrying David Coulthard crashed at Lyon airport today, killing both pilots. Coulthard, his fiancée Heidi Wichlinski, and trainer Andrew Matthews survived. [See feature opposite]

WHEN DAVID COULTHARD LEFT Farnborough airport in southern England at midday on Tuesday, 2 May, to return to his home in Monaco, he had no idea of the drama to follow. The Learjet chartered by Coulthard was also carrying his fiancée Heidi Wichlinski and personal trainer Andrew Matthews, along with the two pilots, David Saunders and Daniel Worley.

All seemed to be well, until the co-pilot informed the passengers that the aircraft had an engine problem and would divert to Lyon, France, to make an emergency landing.

Ordeal by fire

Coulthard described what happened as the jet came in to land: "We prepared ourselves for the landing in a brace position. On impact the plane's fuel tanks ruptured and there was a fire at the right-hand side of the aircraft. When the plane finally came to a rest, the front of the cockpit had broken free. At this point we established the only way out was through the front of the craft. Andy led the way through the debris."

Once his companions were safely out of the plane, Coulthard returned to see if there was anything he could do for the pilots, but in vain. It was

David Coulthard and his fiancée Heidi Wichlinski, survivors of an air crash on 2 May.

survives death crash

later discovered that Coulthard had cracked three ribs, although he kept this knowledge concealed until after the Spanish Grand Prix despite being in considerable pain.

Controversial decision

Coulthard's decision to drive in the race at Catalunya was a point of controversy, but he said: "I would not be driving if I did not feel totally comfortable with my decision."

Some observers suggested that Coulthard should not participate as a mark of respect for the dead pilots, but he said that he believed they would have wanted him to race. McLaren boss Ron Dennis revealed that the father of one of the pilots had told Coulthard to "put it on pole".

Worried drivers

Coulthard's plane accident caused consternation among other F1 drivers, who use light aircraft on a weekly basis to transport them to races and testing sessions. Benetton driver Giancarlo Fisichella is also a Monaco resident. He and Coulthard, along

Investigators search through the wreckage of the light aircraft which crashed with Coulthard on board.

with fellow drivers Alexander Wurz and Pedro Diniz, sometimes share leasing costs on an aircraft. "It could quite easily have been me on board the plane," said Fisichella. "A month ago, David gave me a ride from Jerez to Monte Carlo, and I think it was the same plane. We have to consider that we spend our F1 lives constantly getting on and off planes."

Close calls

Both Eddie Irvine and Michael Schumacher experienced close calls in the air last season, with the German driver's Challenger jet forced to make an emergency landing after a fire broke out in mid-flight. But Formula One drivers are focused men, and have learnt to live with danger on and off the track. As Coulthard explained: "Driving is the most important thing for me – it's what I get up for in the morning."

What is going wrong at Jaguar?

The leaping cat has failed to pounce so far this season, damaging rather than enhancing the Jaguar image.

AFTER THE STEWART TEAM'S good run in the 1999 season, great things were expected of them in 2000, rebadged as Jaguar. But despite the injection of Ford money and know-how, Jaguar have performed quite miserably. Both their drivers failed to finish in the first two grand prixs, and their best showing after four races was seventh place for Eddie Irvine at Imola.

In part Jaguar's troubles stem from the disruption of the close-knit Stewart set-up. This problem was compounded when Paul Stewart stepped down for medical reasons.

Changing places

Ford have tried to solve the problem with a managerial reshuffle that has seen Jaguar chairman Neil Ressler take over Stewart's job, with extra input from other top Ford executives.

Another difficulty facing Jaguar is the scattered nature of their operation. The main factory is in Milton Keynes, Buckinghamshire, while the Cosworth engines come from Northamptonshire. But much engine testing is done in Detroit, Michigan, and the wind-tunnel is in California.

Jaguar have announced that they intend to build a new factory to house the whole manufacturing and testing process under a single roof. The new Jaguar headquarters, which will probably be sited near Silverstone, will include the all-important (and highly expensive) wind-tunnel. It will be at least two years, however, before the new factory is up and running. Until then, Jaguar must find some other way of improving results.

7 MAY • BARCELONA
Spanish Grand Prix

In a grand prix **full of dramatic incident,** Ferrari **fumbled** in the pits, the **Schumacher brothers** clashed, and **McLaren** celebrated **maximum** points.

Race Result

	Driver	Time
1	Hakkinen	1:33.55.390
2	Coulthard	1:34.11.456
3	Barrichello	1:34.24.502
4	R. Schumacher	1:34.32.701
5	M. Schumacher	1:34.43.373
6	Frentzen	1:35.17.315

Drivers' Championship

	Driver	Points
1	M. Schumacher	36
2	Hakkinen	22
3	Coulthard	20
4	Barrichello	13
5	R. Schumacher	12
6	Fisichella	8
7	Frentzen	5
	=Villeneuve	5
9	Trulli	4

Button, 3 points. Salo, Zonta, 1 point.

Constructors' Championship

	Constructor	Points
1	Ferrari	49
2	McLaren	42
3	Williams	15
4	Jordan	9
5	Benetton	8
6	BAR	6
7	Sauber	1

The Circuit

The Circuit de Catalunya presents few overtaking opportunities, which has on occasion led to some dull grand prixs. However, it is popular with the drivers from a safety point of view. The circuit imposes heavy demands on drivers' fitness and on the cars, which are subject to high levels of fuel consumption and tyre wear, the latter a consequence of the track's highly abrasive surface. The drivers are extremely familiar with the circuit because it is used extensively for winter testing.

Track length 4.727 km (2.937 miles)
Race distance 307.255 km (190.905 miles) — 65 laps
1999 winner Mika Hakkinen, McLaren
Lap record 1:22.242 min, Giancarlo Fisichella, Jordan-Peugeot, 1997

Mika Hakkinen and his rival Michael
Schumacher both enter the pits.

Brave Coulthard inspires McLaren resurgence

Qualification

Last year's Ferrari built up an enviable reputation for reliability, but this year's F1-2000 model has proved fast as well. At Catalunya it allowed Michael Schumacher deftly to snatch pole from Hakkinen – although Schumacher was probably helped by going out for his best lap when passing cloud cover briefly lowered the track temperature. A cooler track generally improves qualifying times.

Ralf puts down Jenson

The two title-contending teams took the four top places, although Ralf Schumacher impressed with his BMW-Williams, which was only a tenth of a second behind fourth-placed Coulthard. The younger Schumacher's performance must have been especially satisfying as he had clearly outpaced his team-mate Jenson Button, who languished in 11th place. It was sweet revenge for Button's qualifying ahead of Schumacher junior at Silverstone.

Villeneuve managed to coax some extra speed out of his Honda-powered BAR to take sixth place, gaining the edge over the Mugen-Hondas of Jordan which occupied the fourth row of the grid.

Qualifying Times

1	M. Schumacher	Ferrari	1:20.974
2	Hakkinen	McLaren	1:21.052
3	Barrichello	Ferrari	1:21.416
4	Coulthard	McLaren	1:21.422
5	R. Schumacher	Williams	1:21.605
6	Villeneuve	BAR	1:21.963
7	Trulli	Jordan	1:22.006
8	Frentzen	Jordan	1:22.135
9	De la Rosa	Arrows	1:22.185*
10	Irvine	Jaguar	1:22.370
11	Button	Williams	1:22.385
12	Verstappen	Arrows	1:22.421
13	Salo	Sauber	1:22.443
14	Fisichella	Benetton	1:22.569
15	Herbert	Jaguar	1:22.781
16	Diniz	Sauber	1:22.841
17	Zonta	BAR	1:22.882
18	Alesi	Prost	1:22.894
19	Wurz	Benetton	1:23.010
20	Heidfeld	Prost	1:23.033
21	Gené	Minardi	1:23.486
22	Mazzacane	Minardi	1:24.257

*De la Rosa was sent to the back of the grid because of a fuel irregularity.

American writer Ernest Hemingway once defined courage as "grace under pressure", an apt description of David Coulthard's superb second-place drive at Catalunya. Besides the trauma of his recent air crash, Coulthard drove with three cracked ribs which caused him intense pain for much of the race. And McLaren gained further satisfaction as Hakkinen took his first chequered flag of the season.

Coulthard shows the strain of racing only five days after a plane crash.

At the lights, Michael Schumacher got away smoothly from pole position, with Hakkinen in pursuit and the rest of the field well behind. Hakkinen's only hope of passing Schumacher was to wait calmly for a pit-stop, and on lap 24 the Ferrari driver duly obliged.

Pit-stop mayhem

The pit-stop seemed to be going well for Schumacher until the lollipop man gave the signal to go a fraction of a second too early, before the chief mechanic Nigel Stepney had fully disengaged the fuel hose. As a result, Schumacher inadvertently ran over the unfortunate Stepney's leg. Despite the incident, Schumacher was able to resume the lead after Hakkinen completed his first stop.

Schumacher and Hakkinen came in together for their second stops on lap 41. The injured Stepney had been replaced by a less experienced team-mate who had difficulty engaging the fuel nozzle. Schumacher sat quietly in his private hell for a full 17.5 seconds, watching Hakkinen drive past him up the pit lane and out on to the track.

Making his first pit-stop, Schumacher accelerates away too soon, before the Ferrari fuel crew have had time to move away from the car.

Worse was to follow. Schumacher had been one of the few drivers to choose harder compound tyres, and even before coming in for his second stop it had seemed likely that he might lose the lead. Once back on the track, his tyre problems worsened, culminating in a slow puncture.

Coulthard was soon closing in on Schumacher, having overtaken Barrichello and Schumacher junior during the second round of pit-stops.

Coulthard was clearly the faster driver but Schumacher made his Ferrari as wide as possible, balking the Scot's attempts to get past. When on lap 47 Coulthard committed himself and went to pass on the inside at 180 mph, Schumacher cut across his path. On the following lap, however, Coulthard overtook the Ferrari on the outside.

Unfair manoeuvre

Schumacher's tactics had infuriated Coulthard. "I didn't feel the first move was fair," he said. "He waited until I was fully committed and had the momentum. We almost collided. It was extremely close, and it was a relief to get away with it." But the German driver rebutted Coulthard's criticisms: "The rules state you are allowed to change your line once," he said, "and that's exactly what I did."

The battling pair of Barrichello and Ralf Schumacher also began to overhaul Michael Schumacher. On lap 50 the Ferrari number one pushed his brother wide as they fought for third place, letting Barrichello slip through. Ralf was galled by Michael's antics, and made his feelings clear to his brother after the race.

Hakkinen crossed the finish line comfortably ahead of Coulthard. On the podium, the Finn celebrated his first win of the year. But an exhausted and reflective David Coulthard took his trophy and quietly slipped away.

Hakkinen treats Barrichello to a champagne shower.

Above: Hit by the rear wheel, chief mechanic Nigel Stepney rolls
on the ground. Above right: Stepney is led away by colleagues.

Main picture: Hakkinen powers to his
first win of the season, a comfortable
victory in the end as Schumacher's
difficulties accumulated.

BETWEEN THE RACES

9 May *Peace talks between F1 and EU imminent*

The long-running dispute between the European Union and the FIA, Formula One's governing body, may be coming to a close. The EU had accused the FIA of exercising an illegal monopoly over the sport.

After four years of threats and counter-threats a compromise solution has been proposed by FIA president Max Mosley. Although Mosley refused to disclose details of the proposals, they are thought to involve the FIA withdrawing from the commercial side of the sport in favour of a largely regulatory role.

EU competition commissioner Mario Monti described Mosley's proposals as "innovative and constructive". He is to arrange a meeting with representatives of the FIA in the near future.

10 May *EM.TV increases grip on Formula One*

Thomas Haffa, the German TV mogul who bought half of Formula One's commercial organization, the FOA, earlier this year, intends to exercise his option to buy a further 25 per cent of the company. This means that Bernie Ecclestone will lose his

FIA president Max Mosley is looking for a compromise with the European Union.

Flavio Briatore would like to see some radical innovations in Formula One.

controlling interest in the FOA. Haffa says, however, that he has no intention of attempting to remove Ecclestone from his dominant role in F1: "I want him to continue the dynamic impact he has today, and run the show as long as possible." Haffa has stated that he intends to float the company on the stock exchange within the next 18 months.

11 May *Briatore calls for changes to race weekends*

The recently returned Benetton boss Flavio Briatore has criticized the present organization of race weekends. Briatore believes that Friday practice should be dropped or combined with the Saturday qualifying session. "There is no need for Friday running, as nobody wants to go

out on the track," said Briatore. "If the powers-that-be insist on the Friday session then the times should be added to the Saturday qualifying session so that you arrive at an aggregate."

15 May *Wurz's position in jeopardy*

Benetton driver Alexander Wurz is unlikely to hold his place in the team after the end of the year. The lanky Austrian has had a poor season so far, and has been censured by new team boss Flavio Briatore for his failure to match up to the performance of his team-mate Giancarlo Fisichella. The Italian driver has notched up eight points in five races, while Wurz's best finish has been a seventh place at Melbourne. Benetton have made no secret of wishing to tempt

former world champion Jacques Villeneuve away from BAR, although the young Brazilian driver Antonio Pizzonia, currently in F3, has also been involved in talks with Benetton.

17 May *Ralf slams Rubens*

Rubens Barrichello has been criticized by Ralf Schumacher for allegedly not helping brother Michael sufficiently in the battle for the championship. "Barrichello has to stop thinking he's under pressure to beat Michael," said Ralf, "because he has absolutely no chance of competing for the title. He should, instead, be at the disposal of the team in order to help Michael." A bemused Barrichello could only surmise that this outburst was the consequence

Rubens Barrichello is dodging flak from the Schumacher family.

of the incident at Barcelona in which he overtook Ralf to take third place. Ironically, the overtaking move was only made possible by Michael Schumacher pushing his brother aside to let Barrichello through.

18 May *Delayed return for injured Ferrari mechanic*

Ferrari chief mechanic and refueller Nigel Stepney will be out of action until the Canadian Grand Prix. He had his ankle broken when Michael Schumacher struck his leg at the Spanish Grand Prix. Claudio Bisi will become chief mechanic, while Pietro Timpini takes over refuelling.

Alex Wurz flanked by Ricardo Zonta (left) and Jean Alesi — three drivers who are having a difficult season in Formula One.

Men behaving badly on the track

ULTIMATE SUCCESS IN FORMULA One offers riches and fame that few sports can match, and so the battle for the championship can at times be a ruthless contest. Drivers subscribe to a code of conduct that sets limits to acceptable behaviour in the pursuit of victory. But this code is largely unwritten, leaving a wide degree of latitude in its interpretation.

Blocking moves

Overtaking presents the major point of contention. To what degree can a slower driver legitimately block a rival trying to pass him? Holding the racing line is always considered acceptable; the overtaking driver must be ahead of the other car before the latter has to give way. A current ruling states that the leading driver can also attempt to block the overtaking driver on one occasion; after that he must move over.

Driving to the limit

Michael Schumacher is the driver whose name most often crops up in debates over "driver etiquette". This season, for example, he chopped across David Coulthard at the start at Imola, and at Barcelona his blocking tactics against the same McLaren driver pushed the concept of defensive driving to its absolute limit.

Schumacher has a long history of dubious behaviour, dating back to the collision with Damon Hill at Adelaide in 1994, where he took the world title at Hill's expense. This was followed by his infamous unsuccessful attempt to take Jacques Villeneuve off the track in the race at Jerez in 1997.

Schumacher apologized for the Jerez incident, but cited in his defence the example of Ayrton Senna and Alain Prost. The collisions between the two drivers at Suzuka in 1989 and 1990 certainly did nothing to enhance the reputation of Formula One. In 1989, Prost refused to move over as Senna attempted to pass him, taking both drivers off the track, and in the following year's race, Senna simply ran into Prost to take the world title.

Changing values

Such behaviour, which was almost unknown in the 1950s and 1960s, is partly a reflection of changing values in sport. It may also be to some extent a consequence of progress in car safety, which now allows drivers to

Above: Senna rams Prost's Ferrari at Suzuka in 1990; both cars went off, leaving Senna as champion.

ram each other off the track with little chance of serious injury.

The FIA has traditionally taken a relaxed attitude to driver conduct. FIA president Max Mosley has publicly defended Schumacher's recent conduct. But if the Ferrari driver continues to weave across the track, other drivers may take action of their own to counter his unsportsmanlike tactics.

Left: Schumacher, F1 "bad guy"? Right: Schuey's car is lifted away after his collision with Villeneuve at Jerez in 1997.

European Grand Prix

The Circuit

Today's Nürburgring occupies an area of the Nordschliefe circuit in the Eifel mountains, which for 50 years was the world's most spectacular and dangerous course. The modern track is designed for Formula One racing; the tight Castrol S bend just after the finishing line is the scene of many mishaps, and the bends at RTL and Coca Cola also provide excitement.

Track length 4.556 km
(2.831 miles)
Race distance 305.252 km
(189.677 miles) — 67 laps
1999 winner Johnny Herbert,
Stewart-Ford
Lap record 1:18.805 min,
Heinz-Harald Frentzen,
Williams-Renault, 1997

Race Result

	Driver	Time
1	M. Schumacher	1:42.00.307
2	Hakkinen	1:42.14.129
3	Coulthard	1 lap behind
4	Barrichello	1 lap behind
5	Fisichella	1 lap behind
6	De la Rosa	1 lap behind

Drivers' Championship

	Driver	Points
1	M. Schumacher	46
2	Hakkinen	28
3	Coulthard	24
4	Barrichello	16
5	R. Schumacher	12
6	Fisichella	10
7	Frentzen	5
	=Villeneuve	5
9	Trulli	4

Button, 3 points. De la Rosa, Salo, Zonta, 1 point.

Constructors' Championship

	Constructor	Points
1	Ferrari	62
2	McLaren	52
3	Williams	15
4	Benetton	10
5	Jordan	9
6	BAR	6
7	Arrows	1
	=Sauber	1

Mika Hakkinen is lost in a mist of spray, struggling to pass slower Benetton and Sauber machines.

Schumacher blazed a **path to victory** through torrential rain as **his rival Hakkinen,** in front at the start, **failed to cope** as effectively with the conditions.

Schumacher is the lord of the Ring

Qualification

Intermittent heavy showers made the qualifying session something of a lottery, with rich rewards for a fast lap at just the right moment.

Through the first half of the session, the track was drying and lap times regularly improved. The Ferrari and McLaren drivers leap-frogged one another in successive outings until Coulthard put in a lap of 1:17.529. Michael Schumacher failed to match it by a tenth of a second. Then, with 25 minutes to go, a heavy shower intervened.

Last-ditch effort

Two minutes from the end of the session, as the track dried again, Schumacher re-emerged in a last-ditch effort to snatch pole, but he made a mistake at the Dunlop hairpin and could not beat his own earlier best time.

Remarkably, it was Coulthard's first pole position since the 1998 season. Schumacher afterwards declared himself content with second place — perhaps mindful that no driver had won a grand prix from pole this season. Hakkinen was patently unhappy to find himself in an unfamiliar place on the second rank, alongside Barrichello.

Qualifying Times

1	Coulthard	McLaren	1:17.529
2	M. Schumacher	Ferrari	1:17.667
3	Hakkinen	McLaren	1:17.785
4	Barrichello	Ferrari	1:18.227
5	R. Schumacher	Williams	1:18.515
6	Trulli	Jordan	1:18.612
7	Fisichella	Benetton	1:18.697
8	Irvine	Jaguar	1:18.703
9	Villeneuve	BAR	1:18.742
10	Frentzen	Jordan	1:18.830
11	Button	Williams	1:18.887
12	De la Rosa	Arrows	1:19.024
13	Verstappen	Arrows	1:19.190
14	Wurz	Benetton	1:19.378
15	Diniz	Sauber	1:19.422
16	Herbert	Jaguar	1:19.638
17	Alesi	Prost	1:19.651
18	Zonta	BAR	1:19.766
19	Salo	Sauber	1:19.814
20	Gené	Minardi	1:20.162
21	Mazzacane	Minardi	1:21.015

Heidfeld was disqualified for being under the regulation weight.

Undeterred by wind and rain, the legions of Michael Schumacher fans turned out to see their hero win on his home circuit. Mika Hakkinen did his best to spoil the party, but Schumacher showed again what an outstanding driver he is in wet conditions, pushing his car to the limit in a bravura display of courage and control.

Hakkinen made an electrifying start from third place on the grid, cutting between Coulthard and Schumacher to lead into the first corner. He just brushed against the Ferrari on the way through, a light touch that Schumacher had the ill-grace to complain about after the race.

Duel at the front

Schumacher set off in pursuit of Hakkinen, and from that point on the two leaders conducted a personal duel. The Finn resisted his pursuer as long as the rain held off, but once the track became wet the German pounced. On lap 11, roaring into the Veedol chicane, he passed Hakkinen on the inside. The gentlemanly Finn made no attempt to block.

As the rain thickened, the drivers pitted for wets. Back on the track, with sheets of water on the ground

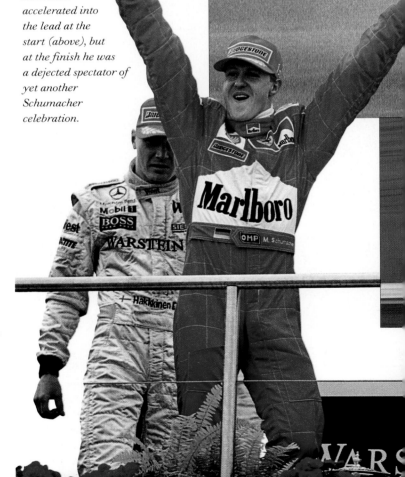

Hakkinen accelerated into the lead at the start (above), but at the finish he was a dejected spectator of yet another Schumacher celebration.

Schumacher, the "rain master", has no equal as a driver in wet conditions.

Above: Pedro de la Rosa speeds on his way to sixth place, a fine performance that brought the first point of the season for Arrows.

and visibility impaired by rain and spray, Schumacher nonetheless set a cracking pace. Hakkinen was still close enough to take over the lead when the German made his second pit-stop, on lap 35. But the Finn soon lost vital seconds in traffic and, by the time it was his turn to pit, he was only 18 seconds ahead. Schumacher duly took back the lead and swept on imperiously to the finish.

Coulthard was surprised to come third. The Scot found his car hard to handle throughout – it was, he later said, "the hardest fight I have ever had to keep the car in a straight line". As for fourth-placed Barrichello, his race was ruined by Ferrari tactical errors that forced him to pit three times.

While the Ferraris and McLarens battled at the front, an eventful scrap full of thrills and spills developed behind them. The Jordan team were reduced to spectators soon after the start: Trulli retired after a collision with Fisichella at the first corner, and Frentzen's engine gave out on lap 3. Further mayhem was inevitable, with many cars running in close formation in the dreadful conditions, and it arrived on lap 30, when Verstappen, Irvine, and Ralf Schumacher came together at the first corner. The British and German drivers went off

immediately, and the damaged Arrows crashed spectacularly a few moments later. Towards the end of the race, Herbert was taken off by Wurz, but the reliable Fisichella held on to collect another two points. De la Rosa, looking impressive throughout, took sixth place for Arrows.

Superior rivals

There was no doubting the absolute superiority of Schumacher and Hakkinen on the day. By the finish they had lapped every other car at least once. But it was little consolation for the Finn to have been such a good second, as he saw his rival stretch his drivers' championship lead to an impressive 18 points.

Schumacher was understandably jubilant: "This is the sort of start to the season I only dreamt of," he said. "It shows that dreams can come true."

23 May *Traction-control cheats escape punishment*

The FIA has decided not to attempt a prosecution of the team they think was illegally using black-box technology as a traction-control aid during last season. After sifting through reams of software data, downloaded from the engine control unit of what is believed to be a mid-table team, the FIA remains certain that cheating took place but lacks the evidence to launch a successful prosecution. News of the affair was made known at the San Marino Grand Prix, and led to revised software and new checking procedures at the British Grand Prix.

24 May *Fisichella and Trulli collide once again*

After a coming together at the European Grand Prix, Giancarlo Fisichella and Jarno Trulli have collided again during testing at Valencia. Travelling at high speed, Fisichella's Benetton ran into the back of Trulli's Jordan, which was on a slow out-lap. The Benetton was thrown into the air and flipped over before coming to a halt in the gravel trap the right way up. Although the Benetton was virtually destroyed, the only injury to either of the drivers was a slightly bruised thumb suffered by Fisichella.

The accident will not improve relations between the two Italian drivers, already acrimonious after the earlier incident at the Nürburgring. Trulli was incensed that Fisichella, who went into the back of his Jordan at the first corner, had refused to accept the blame for the collision.

24 May *Hakkinen dismisses Coulthard's driving*

Relations between the two McLaren drivers have become strained after Mika Hakkinen said that his team-mate had reached his limit in terms of pace and could not go any faster. Coulthard, who has been suffering from cracked ribs which, he claims, have affected his performance, reacted sharply to Hakkinen's comments. "Mika is entitled to his opinion," he said, "and, naturally, it is not one I share. I am very disappointed after everything I have done for him."

29 May *Speeding Button busted by French police*

Williams driver Jenson Button has been stopped for speeding while driving near Montpellier in southern France. Button's BMW 330 diesel was clocked at 228 km/h (142 mph), and the driver received a warning and a 5000 franc on-the-spot fine. Despite his status as an F1 driver, the 20-year-old Button is only allowed to drive diesel motors in France. While not in any way condoning the offence, BMW are thought to be quietly pleased at an incident that may have raised the sporting profile of their diesel range.

29 May *Montoya wins Indy 500*

Colombian driver Juan Pablo Montoya has become the first rookie driver in 34 years to win the Indy 500. Having won the CART championship in his first year last season, Montoya is being touted as a potential racing great. His contract with the Chip Ganassi team extends to the end of next year, but it is an open secret that Williams would like to bring him over to Formula One.

Montoya apparently remains unfazed by the fevered speculation surrounding his future. "I hear many things," he said, "and, yes, Formula One has always been my goal. All I know is that I've got a contract with Chip for next year. I'm not in any hurry, either. The opportunity has to be right for me to go."

Fisichella crashes during testing in Valencia; he climbed out of the car virtually unscathed (inset).

Backroom boys in the limelight

Juan Montoya celebrates winning the Indy 500 at the first attempt. Does his future lie in Formula One?

IN RECENT YEARS THE DESIGNER has emerged from the shadows to be recognized as a major player in the world of motor racing. McLaren's Adrian Newey, for example, is seen as a key influence in winning two world championships for Mika Hakkinen and well worth a reputed salary of around £2 million a year.

Design amateurs

Yet design once tended to be the preserve of team owners, who were often former drivers, such as John Cooper and Jack Brabham. They would outline overall principles, while the engineers would actually construct the cars. Lotus owner Colin Chapman was at the forefront of design in the 1960s and 1970s, introducing the first monocoque chassis in 1962 and the ground-effect car in 1977.

It was in the 1980s that dedicated designers began to play an important role within the F1 hierarchy. Ligier designer Frank Dernie caused a stir when he demanded a reported annual fee of £400,000 for his services, confirming, in a world where cash is king, the elevation of the designer to royal status. He was followed by John Barnard, who at McLaren established himself as a design guru, known and respected by all within F1 — and able to command a price to match.

New responsibilities

In the 1990s, the greater complexity of Formula One designs — where sketches on the backs of envelopes had been superseded by CAD-CAM projections — extended the scope and responsibilities of the designer, opening the way for the emergence of a new role, "technical director".

Patrick Head of Williams is an example of a man who started off as a straightforward designer but now has the title of technical director, with responsibility for the management of all technical aspects of the team. Under him are chief designer Gavin Fisher and aerodynamicist Geoff Willis, working alongside Gerhard Berger of engine supplier BMW.

Top to bottom: John Barnard, once of McLaren, now with Prost; Patrick Head, design guru at Williams since the 1970s; and Adrian Newey of Mclaren.

A similar situation exists at Ferrari, where former designer Ross Brawn has found himself increasingly involved in more general technical matters, notably overseeing race tactics, leaving design to Rory Byrne.

Today's designer or technical director occupies a position not unlike that of the drivers — highly paid and liable to be poached by another ambitious team. This year, Jordan technical director Mike Gascoyne was snapped up by Benetton-Renault, despite a contract lasting until the summer of 2001.

But if a team performs poorly, then the designer can find himself cast as a scapegoat — as Alan Jenkins found out when things went pear-shaped at Prost this season.

4 JUNE • MONTE CARLO

Monaco Grand Prix

Despite its **matchless setting**, this year's Monaco race was far more about **grind** than **glamour** – with David Coulthard worthy winner in a **test of endurance.**

The Circuit

The street-circuit race that winds through the centre of Monte Carlo is one of the high points of the grand prix season. No other circuit demands quite such a high level of concentration. With hardly any run-off areas, the slightest mistake can result in a damaging collision with the crash barriers. Overtaking is almost impossible.

Track length 3.366 km (2.092 miles)
Race distance 262.548 km (163.176 miles) – 78 laps
1999 winner Michael Schumacher, Ferrari
Lap record 1:22.259 min, Mika Hakkinen, McLaren-Mercedes, 1999

Race Result

	Driver	Time
1	Coulthard	1:49.28.213
2	Barrichello	1:49.44.102
3	Fisichella	1:49.46.735
4	Irvine	1:50.34.137
5	Salo	1:50.48.988
6	Hakkinen	1 lap behind

Drivers' Championship

	Driver	Points
1	M. Schumacher	46
2	Coulthard	34
3	Hakkinen	29
4	Barrichello	22
5	Fisichella	14
6	R. Schumacher	12
7	Frentzen	5
	=Villeneuve	5
9	Trulli	4

Button, Irvine, Salo, 3 points. De la Rosa, Zonta, 1 point.

Constructors' Championship

	Constructor	Points
1	Ferrari	68
2	McLaren	63
3	Williams	15
4	Benetton	14
5	Jordan	9
6	BAR	6
7	Jaguar	3
	=Sauber	3
9	Arrows	1

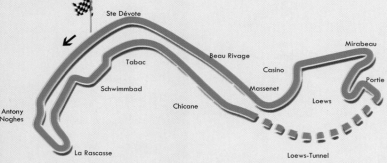

Mika Salo sweeps along the harbourfront, on his way to fifth place.

Coulthard profits as Ferrari's luck runs out

Qualification

Monte Carlo is known as one of Michael Schumacher's favourite circuits, and the fact that the Ferrari driver secured pole was hardly surprising. But the performance of the Jordans, qualifying second and fourth, was another matter.

Jordan had previously failed to build on last year's excellent results, but Trulli drove superbly, laying down two provisional poles before being clipped by Schumacher towards the end of the session. Frentzen was just two-tenths of a second behind his colleague.

Frustrated Finn

Coulthard was a little dissatisfied to find himself in third place, but his disappointment was nothing to that of his team-mate Hakkinen. The short, winding circuit tends to produce traffic jams, and every time the Finn attempted a flying lap, someone or something was in his way. A few minutes before the end of the session Hakkinen was in 17th place, and only a reasonably clear last run enabled him to climb up to a moderately respectable fifth.

Just behind him were Barrichello and Alesi. The French driver impressed most observers with an excellent seventh place for Prost.

Qualifying Times

1	M. Schumacher	Ferrari	1:19.475
2	Trulli	Jordan	1:19.746
3	Coulthard	McLaren	1:19.888
4	Frentzen	Jordan	1:19.961
5	Hakkinen	McLaren	1:20.241
6	Barrichello	Ferrari	1:20.416
7	Alesi	Prost	1:20.494
8	Fisichella	Benetton	1:20.703
9	R. Schumacher	Williams	1:20.742
10	Irvine	Jaguar	1:20.743
11	Herbert	Jaguar	1:20.792
12	Wurz	Benetton	1:20.871
13	Salo	Sauber	1:21.561
14	Button	Williams	1:21.605
15	Verstappen	Arrows	1:21.738
16	De la Rosa	Arrows	1:21.832
17	Villeneuve	BAR	1:21.848
18	Heidfeld	Prost	1:22.017
19	Diniz	Sauber	1:22.136
20	Zonta	BAR	1:22.324
21	Gené	Minardi	1:23.721
22	Mazzacane	Minardi	1:23.794

David Coulthard has had more than his fair share of misfortune, but in winning at Monaco he seized whatever luck was going as others around him — including Michael Schumacher — fell by the wayside. The quality of Coulthard's drive could not be faulted, displaying both patience and controlled aggression. On a circuit that ruthlessly punishes mistakes, he did not put a foot wrong from start to finish.

The race began as farce, with delay following delay. First time round, Wurz's Benetton began to belch smoke from a blown engine, while the second start was aborted when Pedro de la Rosa's Arrows attempted to nose past the Williams of Jenson Button at the Loews hairpin. It was an over-ambitious move and the cars became tangled, blocking the road with nearly half the field stuck behind them.

Spectators then witnessed the bizarre sight of a gaggle of drivers sprinting back to the pits in an attempt to get into their spare cars for the restart.

Schuey in command

At the third attempt they got away cleanly, with pole-placed Michael Schumacher ahead of Jarno Trulli, Coulthard, Frentzen, and Hakkinen. As Schumacher began to build up a commanding lead, Coulthard found himself stuck behind Trulli. The Scottish driver was clearly faster, but unable to get past the Jordan. On lap 37, however, luck came Coulthard's way when Trulli's gearbox failed. The Scot buried the accelerator and put in a series of swift laps, beginning to draw closer to Schumacher.

Nevertheless, Coulthard's chances of actually getting past Schumacher still seemed remote when, on lap 56, the Ferrari suddenly slowed, the victim of suspension failure. After Schumacher had piloted the car back to the pits, the Ferrari team explained that a cracked exhaust had allowed hot gasses to deform the left rear

Villeneuve was one of several drivers who had to sprint back to the pits in the course of the race weekend.

pushrod. However, both Villeneuve and Salo reported seeing the German driver clip the barrier, suggesting a possible alternative explanation.

Six points lost

As Coulthard deftly drove towards the chequered flag, he was followed by the Jordan of Heinz-Harald Frentzen, who seemed sure of six points. But on lap 71 Frentzen over-braked coming into Sainte Dévote, bringing his race to a premature end. Eddie Jordan was philosophical about the disastrous weekend. Of Frentzen's error, Jordan said: "He came and apologized, so what else can you say? We all make mistakes in this business."

Frentzen's accident was only one of several incidents at Sainte Dévote; the other victims of uncertain grip included Wurz and Ralf Schumacher, the latter badly gashing his leg as he smashed into the barrier.

The high rate of attrition that is standard for Monaco gave hope to any who could simply last the race. After a poor start, Barrichello drove steadily to take second place, closely followed by Fisichella's Benetton. Irvine's fourth place gave a relieved Jaguar their first points of the season after seven races.

Mika holds off Mika

The last two points positions were taken by the two Mikas, Salo's Sauber leading Hakkinen's McLaren over the line. Overall, Hakkinen had a grim weekend. Having been balked in qualifying, during the race itself he was plagued by technical gremlins. First, brake problems forced him to

take his pit-stop early so the fault could be rectified. Then, after he had laid down a series of fastest laps, fighting his way back to sixth, any hope he had of getting past Salo was ended by gearbox problems, which forced him to ease off and accept the single point. "All in all," reflected Hakkinen, "I was lucky to get that."

Hakkinen's fortuitous point was not enough to prevent Coulthard leap-frogging over him in the drivers' championship table to head McLaren's pursuit of Michael Schumacher.

Below right: David Coulthard trails Jarno Trulli around the circuit during the first half of the race. Below left and bottom: Coulthard revels in the experience of his first victory at Monte Carlo.

BETWEEN THE RACES

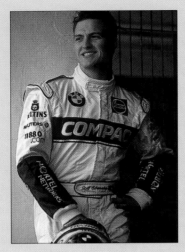

Ralf Schumacher suffered a nasty leg injury in his shunt at Monte Carlo.

5 June Schumacher Junior is doubtful for Canadian GP

Williams driver Ralf Schumacher has only a 50-50 chance of racing in the Canadian Grand Prix in two weeks time. He suffered a badly cut leg when his car crashed into the barrier at Sainte Dévote on lap 37 of the Monaco Grand Prix. The injury was caused by the driver's front wishbone penetrating his calf. The deep cut required several stitches at the nearby Grace Kelly hospital.

12 June Salo came fifth despite steering failure

During testing at Monza, Finnish driver Mika Salo revealed that he was in pain as a result of the power steering on his Sauber failing during the Monaco Grand Prix. Salo raced around the narrow street circuit for most of the race without power steering, which caused severe bruising to his hands. But the Finn's discomfort was compensated for by his excellent fifth place, just ahead of compatriot and rival Mika Hakkinen.

15 June Alesi suggests a new aerodynamic approach

The frustration felt by French driver Jean Alesi at the disappointing performance of his Prost car has spilled over into sarcastic invective:

"Give me a few pieces of wool to stick on the car and a good gust of Mistral wind," Alesi commented, "and I could come up with a better aerodynamic package on the bridge of Avignon than the team has managed.".

The departure of designer Alan Jenkins before the Monaco Grand Prix has caused further confusion within the Prost team, which is yet to score a point this year. However, team boss Alain Prost remains resolutely upbeat, at least in public: "I am confidant in our existing technical staff," he told the press, "and I look forward to a productive future."

Jean Alesi is sadly frustrated at Prost.

17 June New GP for Egypt?

Egypt may be the next grand prix venue for Formula One, and could make its debut as early as 2002. A meeting that included Bernie Ecclestone, Egyptian representative Ashraf Mahmoud, and circuit designer Hermann Tilke discussed building a circuit near Cairo. A grand prix in an Arab country would fit in with Ecclestone's ambition to extend the global reach of F1. For climatic reasons it would have to be staged at the beginning or end of the season.

17 June Villeneuve could move to Benetton-Renault

Jacques Villeneuve has been offered a two-year deal to drive with Benetton-Renault next year. The deal would reportedly be worth $35 million. The French-Canadian driver has repeatedly expressed the wish to drive in a competitive team, and unless BAR can dramatically raise their game it seems highly likely that he will move on at the end of the season.

Villeneuve has expressed strong interest in the Benetton deal but is in no hurry to sign on the dotted line just yet, preferring to let Benetton and BAR fight for his services. If Villeneuve makes the move, it is almost certain that he will replace Alexander Wurz. The empty seat at BAR might be offered to Wurz in a straight swap, although Jenson Button could be a stronger contender if he loses his place at Williams to Montoya.

17 June Sauber supplier line-up confirmed

The Swiss team Sauber are to take up the option of using Ferrari engines next year, although they will conform to this season's specification. At present, there is a shortage of engine suppliers in Formula One, and despite the high cost of the Ferrari engines Sauber will be relieved to have secured a powerful and reliable powerplant. Sauber have also confirmed a deal with Bridgestone to use their tyres and have extended their key sponsorship deal with the cash-rich Malaysian oil company Petronas.

Jacques Villeneuve is a driver in demand, but he could still decide to stay at BAR.

Is Monaco

THE MONACO GRAND PRIX HOLDS a unique place in the racing calendar. It is the only genuine street circuit in F1, wending its way through the narrow and twisting roads of Monte Carlo. But what really makes it special is the aura of glamour associated with the event – the harbour jammed with oversize motor-launches, the casino, the azure blue sky – and its place in the international jet-set season, complete with hordes of "beautiful people" savouring the atmosphere.

Street processions

Yet, for all its glitzy appeal, Monaco is a racing anachronism and arguably does not deserve to be a modern F1 circuit. Although some drivers enjoy the challenge of racing through narrow streets, others dislike the circuit, which makes overtaking all but impossible and tends to lead to dull processional races.

The teams suffer most, however, as the absence of adequate space in the pits and paddock makes it difficult to prepare the cars, while mechanics are forced to carry out tyre changes dangerously close to the pit lane.

This year's race also revealed other shortcomings: the first-lap collision at Loews highlighted the problem of car recovery from the

behind the times as a grand prix venue?

track, and there was also the inability of drivers to return to their garages without the indignity of a long run in their helmets and overalls.

Poor facilities

The circuit has often been criticized by the teams, so it was no surprise that McLaren boss Ron Dennis weighed in against Monaco this year. He called the facilities "third world" and argued that, given the massive sums of money made from the race, the organizers could do much better.

Replying to Dennis's remarks, Bernie Ecclestone commented: "The organizers have done a fantastic job here, considering it is a race in the middle of a city. If we want to be here, then this is the way it has to be."

Commercial reality

Improvements to the circuit facilities are in fact planned, including a new harbour complex, but they will not be completed for several years. Whether these planned improvements really do reduce pit-lane problems is, however, probably irrelevant.

As team boss Sir Frank Williams explained: "The commercial reality is that Monaco is a major attraction for

The overcrowded pit area at Monte Carlo has been criticized by drivers used to better arrangements elsewhere.

the sport's sponsors. We are a show business. The world loves us to perform here, and the people that pay us want us to perform here. That is where the money is."

The sale of television rights is the single most important factor in the global success of Formula One, and

intimately tied up in the overall equation is sponsorship. If the major sponsors want to be in Monaco, then its place on the racing calendar is in effect assured. A Formula One season without a dash through the streets of Monte Carlo remains for the moment virtually unthinkable.

Main picture: Monte Carlo on race day – a scene of glitz and glamour, but also inconvenient and producing some dull processional races.

18 JUNE • MONTREAL
Canadian Grand Prix

The Circuit

On Montreal's Circuit Gilles Villeneuve, long, high-speed straights alternate with slow chicanes and hairpin bends. This shape of racing circuit puts an especially heavy strain on the brakes. However, the long straights before the bends offer good possibilities for overtaking.

Track length 4.421 km (2.747 miles)
Race distance 305.049 km (189.543 miles) — 69 laps
1999 winner Mika Hakkinen, McLaren
Lap record 1:19.379 min, Michael Schumacher, Ferrari, 1998

Race Result

	Driver	Time
1	M. Schumacher	1:41.12.313
2	Barrichello	1:41.12.487
3	Fisichella	1:41.27.678
4	Hakkinen	1:41.30.874
5	Verstappen	1:42.04.521
6	Trulli	1:42.14.000

Drivers' Championship

	Driver	Points
1	M. Schumacher	56
2	Coulthard	34
3	Hakkinen	32
4	Barrichello	28
5	Fisichella	18
6	R. Schumacher	12
7	Frentzen	5
	=Villeneuve	5
	=Trulli	5

Button, Irvine, Salo, 3 points. Verstappen, 2 points. De la Rosa, Zonta, 1 point.

Constructors' Championship

	Constructor	Points
1	Ferrari	84
2	McLaren	66
3	Benetton	18
4	Williams	15
5	Jordan	10
6	BAR	6

Arrows, Jaguar, Sauber, 3 points.

Pits Hairpin

Pont de la Concorde

Virage du Casino

Virage Senna

Michael Schumacher raises a gloved fist, his habitual gesture of victory.

The **first driver** this season to win from **pole position,** Schumacher cruised to his **fifth win** of the year to keep his **commanding lead** in the race for the **drivers' title.**

Coulthard pays a heavy penalty

McLaren's 500th grand prix should have been cause for celebration, but a mere three points for Mika Hakkinen deflated the party balloon as a Ferrari one-two stretched out Schumacher's lead to 22 points. It was little consolation for the Silver Arrows to know that David Coulthard might have seriously challenged Schumacher but for a stop-go penalty.

Qualification

The Ferraris and McLarens claimed the top four places on the grid, again underlining the dominance of the two top teams this season. Towards the end of last year there seemed a possibility that some of the "best-of-the-rest" might be poised to take them on, but instead the performance gap widened.

The only surprise of the top four placings was that Hakkinen was last. The super-qualifier seemed out of sorts in Canada, although McLaren claimed his lack of pace was due to a faulty shock absorber.

Boost for BAR

Of the other teams, BAR impressed with Villeneuve, on his home circuit, sixth and Zonta a very creditable eighth. Villeneuve was sandwiched between the Jordans of Frentzen (fifth) and Trulli (seventh). The test for both Jordan and BAR would be to convert grid positions into points.

Williams had a poor qualifying session, their cars unable to come to terms with the Gilles Villeneuve circuit. Jaguar failed to capitalize on their points win in Monaco, although Johnny Herbert had the satisfaction of outqualifying Eddie Irvine for the first time this season.

Qualifying Times

1	M. Schumacher	Ferrari	1:18.439
2	Coulthard	McLaren	1:18.537
3	Barrichello	Ferrari	1:18.801
4	Hakkinen	McLaren	1:18.985
5	Frentzen	Jordan	1:19.483
6	Villeneuve	BAR	1:19.544
7	Trulli	Jordan	1:19.581
8	Zonta	BAR	1:19.742
9	De la Rosa	Arrows	1:19.912
10	Fisichella	Benetton	1:19.932
11	Herbert	Jaguar	1:19.954
12	R. Schumacher	Williams	1:20.073
13	Verstappen	Arrows	1:20.107
14	Wurz	Benetton	1:20.113
15	Salo	Sauber	1:20.445
16	Irvine	Jaguar	1:20.500
17	Alesi	Prost	1:20.512
18	Button	Williams	1:20.534
19	Diniz	Sauber	1:20.692
20	Gené	Minardi	1:21.058
21	Heidfeld	Prost	1:21.680
22	Mazzacane	Minardi	1:22.091

Schumacher and Coulthard looked set for a close-fought contest before Coulthard's ten-second penalty.

At the start Schumacher, Coulthard, and Hakkinen all got away cleanly. But at the first corner Hakkinen suddenly slowed, allowing Villeneuve and Barrichello past. From then on, while Schumacher and Coulthard escaped into the distance, Villeneuve held up a queue of frustrated drivers led by Barrichello and Hakkinen. Trapped in fourth and fifth places they had absolutely no chance to mount an attack on the leaders.

Stewards intervene

At the front an epic contest seemed in prospect, with Coulthard close behind Schumacher. But on lap 11 news came through that the McLaren driver had been penalized with a ten-second stop-go penalty. Immediately before the parade lap, Coulthard had stalled his engine and been forced to call over his mechanics to restart the McLaren. The race stewards judged that the pit crew had left the grid too late – that is, after the 15-second pit board.

Coulthard came in to serve his penalty on lap 14. He rejoined the race in tenth place, with any serious hopes of challenging Schumacher dashed.

Barrichello eventually passed the rolling roadblock of Villeneuve's BAR and began to make up lost ground. But for team orders, he might even have gone on to win. The Ferrari team thought that Schumacher had a brake problem and told him to slow, but they also told Barrichello to hold off, a request with which he complied. Schumacher was suitably appreciative: "Rubens is a good man," he said, "and one day I will pay him back."

The race had begun under heavy skies and after 20 laps a light drizzle started to fall. When the drivers came in for their planned single pit-stops around lap 40 the rain was still too light for wets, but as soon as most cars were back on the track the rain began to pour, forcing them to stop again to change tyres. The pit lane became a melee of arrivals and departures.

The rain changed the race, with cars spinning off or chopping across the gravel. Jos Verstappen was the hero of the hour, putting in an aggressive charge that took his Arrows past Wurz and Trulli to an eventual fifth place.

Aggressive driving

Villeneuve, who had fallen back after the pit-stops, also tried to improve his position through some aggressive rain-driving. Fired up by the desire to succeed in front of his home crowd, he came up behind Coulthard and Ralf Schumacher. At the hairpin, he swept past Coulthard only to take the Williams driver off into the gravel trap. Villeneuve climbed out of his car to apologize to Schumacher Junior, an apology that was generously accepted.

The driver who benefited most from the rain was Fisichella, whose Benetton came in late enough to collect rain tyres on his single pit-stop. As a result of this, and fine driving, he was able to claim third place.

Giancarlo Fisichella heads for a second consecutive podium place; he is the only driver who has completed every race so far this season.

Fisichella celebrates his well-deserved third place.

A relieved Barrichello passes Villeneuve after 25 laps during which the slower BAR blocked the Ferrari's progress.

BETWEEN THE RACES

McLaren's

21 June *No ban for Silverstone*

The threat to exclude the British Grand Prix from next year's Formula One calendar has been withdrawn following a meeting of the FIA World Council. After hearing representation from Silverstone, the FIA waived any punishment but demanded that the organizers draw up measures to prevent a repeat of the traffic chaos that plagued this year's British GP.

21 June *Technical changes for 2001 announced*

Details of revised Formula One technical regulations for next season have been released. Among the list of published changes are measures designed to assist taller drivers, including a larger cockpit opening and modifications to the seat back. The drivers' removable seat fittings are to be standardized to allow the seats of all cars to be removed using the same tool, and the internal cockpit cross-section will be enlarged, with 25 mm (1in) of foam padding around the driver's legs.

Another significant change is the requirement that wheels must be attached to the main structure of the car by two cables, rather than the present single cable. This is intended to ensure that, in the event of an accident, a wheel will be less likely to break free of the car.

Eddie Jordan may find that a Honda works engine is the answer to his prayers.

28 June *F1 drivers look forward to the US Grand Prix*

Eddie Irvine and Heinz-Harald Frentzen have both expressed their approval of the new Indianapolis circuit while visiting the United States prior to the Canadian Grand Prix. Irvine said: "America has been missing from the calendar for almost 10 years, and to go back when the circuit is the home of the [Indy] 500 is very exciting."

Frentzen praised the design of the new half-oval, half-road Indianapolis track, predicting that it would be the fastest in Formula One. "It's marvellous," said Frentzen. "We'll be coming out of the last corner at 190 km/h (120 mph) and then it is flat out for two kilometres. There will be plenty of overtaking."

29 June *Honda promise works engine for Jordan*

The Honda Motor Corporation have announced that they will supply Jordan with works engines for next season. BAR will also continue to receive works engines and chassis development technology, but Honda's decision to provide Jordan with engine equality will be seen as a snub to BAR.

The deal will be a tremendous boost to Jordan, who have had to make do with the less powerful Mugen-Honda engine. Jordan will also benefit financially, as Honda will supply the engines without fees, saving an annual bill of around $8 million that the team presently pays to Mugen-Honda. Jordan team owner Eddie Jordan believes the new engine will give Jordan a real chance to compete with McLaren and Ferrari on equal terms next season.

30 June *Stewart tells Irvine that he needs to try harder*

Jackie Stewart has criticized Jaguar driver Eddie Irvine, accusing him of not concentrating sufficiently on his racing. The co-founder of the Stewart racing team and former Jaguar chairman said Irvine had the ability to win races but needed to try harder. "He's got to focus more," said Stewart. "He's got to spend more time on the job than he does right now. I think we've got things we have to do to make ourselves more competitive, but so also must our drivers."

EVEN IF THE RACE RESULT DID NOT go McLaren's way in Canada, it was still the team's 500th grand prix and thus a cause for celebration. McLaren are one of the three most successful teams in F1 history (the other two are Williams and Ferrari). From 500 starts, McLaren have won 125 races, an extraordinary one in four grand prixs contested. They have taken eight constructors' and 11 drivers' titles.

The team's founder, New Zealand driver Bruce McLaren, leaped to prominence in 1959 when he recorded his first grand prix win at the tender age of 22, driving a Cooper-Climax. McLaren was as much an engineer as a driver, and in 1963 he decided to

Eddie Irvine may be devoting too much time to life off the track, says Jackie Stewart.

first 500 GPs – a story of achievement

begin setting up his own team. He first raced a McLaren during the 1966 F1 season, and two years later had the rare satisfaction of winning a grand prix in his own car at Spa.

McLaren after McLaren

Bruce McLaren had joined up with fellow New Zealander Denny Hulme, and during the 1968 season the two drivers gave Lotus a run for their money, the team coming second in the constructors' championship.

Tragically, McLaren was killed in July 1970 while testing at Goodwood. But the team carried on under the McLaren name, and even scaled fresh heights. In 1974 Brazilian driver

Emerson Fittipaldi brought McLaren their first drivers' and constructors' titles, and in 1976 James Hunt won them the drivers' title in one of the tightest and most bitterly contested championships in F1 history.

In 1980 a new era began when a company takeover gave Ron Dennis, the owner of a Formula Two team, a leading role in running McLaren. Dennis brought in top designer John Barnard, signed up Niki Lauda and Alain Prost as his drivers, and went into partnership with TAG to finance a Porsche turbo V6 engine. The combination proved irresistible. From 1984 to 1986, McLaren won three drivers' and two constructors' titles.

In 1988 McLaren found a new engine supplier, Honda, and signed up Ayrton Senna to drive alongside Prost. It was a dream combination. Even after Prost left in 1989 victories kept coming.

Fluctuating fortunes

From 1988 to 1991, McLaren set a new record of four consecutive drivers' and constructors' titles. With the subsequent departure of Honda and of Senna, however, McLaren entered a fallow period in the mid-1990s.

They did not begin to turn their fortunes around until 1997, but when it came the revival was spectacular. After a slow start, the new Mercedes engine proved to be a winner, and with the arrival of Adrian Newey the team had a top-class designer. Mika Hakkinen, who had soldiered on with the team during the mid-1990s without success, was joined by David Coulthard, and in 1998 McLaren were back on top of Formula One. Now they must struggle to stay there.

Main picture: Team boss Ron Dennis (left) celebrates McLaren's 500th grand prix. Below, left to right: Team founder Bruce McLaren; Denny Hulme in a McLaren-Ford, 1973; James Hunt, McLaren world champion in 1976; and the great Ayrton Senna in a McLaren-Honda, 1990.

2 JULY • MAGNY-COURS
French Grand Prix

Magny-Cours

The Circuit

The Circuit de Nevers lies in a rural area between Paris and Lyons. The track is smooth and lacks grip in hot weather conditions. The circuit challenges drivers with a tricky combination of high- and slow-speed corners, and overtaking is notoriously difficult, except at the Adelaide hairpin.

Track length 4.250 km (2.641 miles)
Race distance 306.029 km
(190.152 miles) — 72 laps
1999 winner Heinz-Harald Frentzen, Jordan
Lap record 1:17.070 min, Nigel Mansell,
Williams-Renault, 1992

Race Result

	Driver	Time
1	Coulthard	1:38.06.538
2	Hakkinen	1:38.20.286
3	Barrichello	1:38.37.947
4	Villeneuve	1:39.06.860
5	R. Schumacher	1:39.09.519
6	Trulli	1:39.21.143

Drivers' Championship

	Driver	Points
1	M. Schumacher	56
2	Coulthard	44
3	Hakkinen	38
4	Barrichello	32
5	Fisichella	18
6	R. Schumacher	14
7	Villeneuve	8
8	Trulli	6
9	Frentzen	5

Button, Irvine, Salo, 3 points. Verstappen, 2 points. De la Rosa, Zonta, 1 point.

Constructors' Championship

	Constructor	Points
1	Ferrari	88
2	McLaren	82
3	Benetton	18
4	Williams	17
5	Jordan	11
6	BAR	9

Arrows, Jaguar, Sauber, 3 points.

Lycée
Chicane
Estoril
Grande
Courbe
Imola
Golf
Château
d'Eau
Adelaide

David Coulthard raises his fist in salute after a confident and aggressive drive that put him within 12 points of championship leader Michael Schumacher.

Showing **steely determination** as well as the highest driving skills, **David Coulthard** hunted down and then **passed** both Ferraris on his way to a **famous victory.**

"Mr Nice Guy" shows he has the killer instinct

Qualification

The weather was hot for the qualifying session, raising a fair expectation that the fastest times would be set early on, when the track was at its coolest. With impeccable professionalism, Michael Schumacher produced a blistering first run that his rivals spent the rest of the session trying — and failing — to match.

DC frustrated

David Coulthard had been fastest in practice and seemed most likely to deny Schumacher pole. But, frustratingly, his race car was not ready for the start of the session and he was forced to go out in Hakkinen's T-car. By the time his own car was ready the track was hot. Although he came close to Schumacher's time, he had to be content with second place.

A lacklustre Hakkinen qualified behind Barrichello. Ralf Schumacher took the fifth spot, as Williams recovered some of their early-season form, and Jaguar were pleased with sixth place for Eddie Irvine. Most disappointed were the Prost team, once more performing poorly despite home advantage and recent progress in practice.

Qualifying Times

1	M. Schumacher	Ferrari	1:15.632
2	Coulthard	McLaren	1:15.734
3	Barrichello	Ferrari	1:16.047
4	Hakkinen	McLaren	1:16.050
5	R. Schumacher	Williams	1:16.291
6	Irvine	Jaguar	1:16.399
7	Villeneuve	BAR	1:16.653
8	Frentzen	Jordan	1:16.658
9	Trulli	Jordan	1:16.669
10	Button	Williams	1:16.905
11	Herbert	Jaguar	1:17.176
12	Salo	Sauber	1:17.223
13	De la Rosa	Arrows	1:17.279
14	Fisichella	Benetton	1:17.317
15	Diniz	Sauber	1:17.361
16	Heidfeld	Prost	1:17.374
17	Wurz	Benetton	1:17.408
18	Alesi	Prost	1:17.569
19	Zonta	BAR	1:17.668
20	Verstappen	Arrows	1:17.933
21	Gené	Minardi	1:18.130
22	Mazzacane	Minardi	1:18.302

David Coulthard has often been dismissed as lacking the ruthless will-to-win that a potential F1 champion needs. But at Magny-Cours, in probably the finest drive of his career, he took on Michael Schumacher at his most unscrupulous and beat him. It was a thrilling display of controlled aggression that once more threw the world title race wide open.

Battle was joined between Coulthard and Schumacher from the start. The Scottish driver got away better, but Schumacher reacted by cutting across him, forcing him to slow. Barrichello seized the chance to push up on the outside and Coulthard found himself trailing both the Ferraris.

Fierce tussle

Coulthard later grudgingly conceded that Schumacher's blocking move had been "within the rules as they stand", but it set the tone for the fierce tussle that was to follow.

At first it looked as if the brief excitement of the start would be followed by a dull procession. In line with Ferrari's usual team strategy, Barrichello held up Coulthard to allow Schumacher to stretch his lead. But the German driver failed to open up an impressive gap and Coulthard soon began to pressure the Ferrari number two. By lap 22 the Scot was ready to pounce. First he tried to pass Barrichello on the inside, but the Brazilian shut the door. Coming out of the corner, however, Barrichello ran wide and Coulthard pulled past him. It was the kind of overtaking manoeuvre that F1 fans crave to see. Even better was to come.

Coulthard closed on Schumacher and by lap 32 was on his tail. Two laps later he made an attempt to pass the Ferrari on the outside at the Adelaide hairpin, only for Schumacher to force him wider. Coulthard had to back off or be edged off the track. He showed his anger with vigorous hand gestures, for which he subsequently apologized.

It was an especially exhilarating victory for David Coulthard.

Coulthard expresses his anger with an uncharacteristic rude gesture as Schumacher blocks his passing move.

Schumacher's championship bid wavers as Coulthard applies the pressure.

"I know it was not a sporting thing to do," he said, "but my emotions were running very high." Schumacher, by contrast, was unapologetic about his blocking move, commenting: "David tried to overtake me on the outside. Naturally, I tried to make it difficult for him... It's just normal practice."

The race was at boiling point as Coulthard's pursuit continued. On lap 40 he attacked again. This time, with the briefest of contacts between the two cars, he was through.

Schumacher was visibly less and less happy with his set-up. He was passed by Hakkinen as well before mechanical breakdown ended his race on lap 58. Barrichello, who suffered from a bad second pit-stop that took 16.8 seconds, made little effort to

While all eyes were on the McLaren-Ferrari duel, Jacques Villeneuve coaxed enough speed out of his BAR-Honda to hold a lead over the rest of the field.

challenge the McLarens, holding on for a safe third place as the Silver Arrows coasted home.

Behind the gripping struggle for podium places, some other drivers put in strikingly good performances. Jacques Villeneuve moved into the lead of the following pack with his habitual lightning start and held that position throughout the race. Ralf Schumacher, in contrast, started poorly from fifth place on the grid,

but fought his way back, eventually passing the Jordans of Frentzen and Trulli to take two points..

In the end, however, it was only the dramatic duel at the front that really counted. McLaren's one-two left them a mere six points adrift of Ferrari in the constructors' table, and even Schumacher's lead in the drivers' title race was under threat from Coulthard, still 12 points behind but looking capable of closing the gap.

BETWEEN THE RACES

Behind the

4 July *Michelin raise tyre worries*
Michelin director Pierre Dupasquier has called for new guidelines on tyre wear for next season. At the end of a race tyres will often be so worn away that they resemble slicks. Dupasquier is concerned that, when Michelin join Bridgestone as Formula One tyre suppliers in 2001, there will be some disagreement between the two companies over what degree of tyre wear is acceptable.

Dupasquier commented: "Nobody wants to see a driver winning a grand prix only for someone to say that he is disqualified because there was too much wear on his tyres. We are desperately trying to find a way to prevent that happening."

McLaren boss Ron Dennis, right, is concerned about Hakkinen's form.

Italian circuit is considered to have similar characteristics to the Austrian A-1 Ring. McLaren test driver Olivier Panis was joined on the track by Ferrari's Luca Badoer, the McLaren driver having the slight edge in pace. Michael Schumacher and David Coulthard were also both present, although their only mutual acknowledgement was a wave from

7 July *Out-of-form Hakkinen is told to take a rest*
McLaren boss Ron Dennis has given Mika Hakkinen a break from testing duties and instructed him to take a holiday in order to "recharge his batteries". So far this season Hakkinen has appeared out of sorts, seemingly lacking the motivation that made him a double world champion. At present he is 18 points behind Michael Schumacher, and has won only one race while his team-mate David Coulthard has been victorious three times.

Dennis explained that Hakkinen was "suffering from a bit of psychological tiredness, but it's really of no concern". He continued: "I've made the mistake of not backing off on the driver's duties. As their work is very hard for this part of the season, they need a psychological break. So Mika is having quite a long break now, and David will be taking a holiday after the next race."

10 July *Claim that crime ring was behind DC crash*
Reports in the British press suggest that a Malaysian betting ring may have been behind the recent air crash involving David Coulthard. There are similarities between the Coulthard incident and another air crash this year in which champion jockey Frankie Dettori narrowly escaped death. British police have apparently received a tip-off that both crashes might have been engineered by betting syndicates.

A police source was quoted as saying: "It seems astonishing but our informants insist that this is what has happened, and we are investigating. We know that these gangs have killed people in Asia to pull off gambling coups."

THE FRENCH GRAND PRIX MARKED the halfway point of the Formula One season, a suitable moment to reflect on the failure of any third team to challenge the total dominance of Ferrari and McLaren.

Towards the end of last season, Jordan had given the top two a run for their money, and it seemed they might have the potential to be serious championship contenders. But after nine grand prixs this year Jordan were languishing in fifth place.

Problems at Jordan
One reason for Jordan's failure was a high degree of unreliability: only eight finishes in nine races. The uncertainty caused by technical director Mike Gascoyne's imminent departure to Benetton-Renault did not help team morale. And the drivers had their problems. Frentzen was making more mistakes than usual and at times seemed anonymous, while Trulli took a long time to accustom himself to the new EJ10 car.

Long-term potential
Benetton and Williams, two teams with ambitions to mount a title challenge in the next few seasons, could take some comfort from their first-half performance during 2000. Benetton were beginning to pull themselves out of the trough that followed the departure of Michael Schumacher and Ross Brawn to Ferrari in 1996, although they were too reliant on one driver, Fisichella, who had produced all their points by mid-season while Wurz struggled.

Williams were also gradually working their way back towards the top. The new BMW engine was proving more powerful and reliable than anyone expected, and the FW22 chassis made the car far easier to drive. Ralf Schumacher continued to demonstrate his ability as a world-class driver, while Jenson Button had proved something of a revelation.

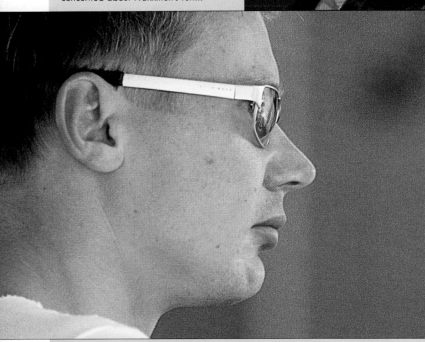

World champion Mika Hakkinen seems tired and lacking in motivation.

5 July *McLaren enter Ferrari country*
In a surprise move, McLaren tested today at the Ferrari-owned circuit of Mugello. McLaren paid a substantial sum for the privilege, which came as part of their preparations for the forthcoming Austrian Grand Prix – the

Coulthard. When questioned about McLaren's decision to test at Mugello, technical director Adrian Newey was unconcerned. "As far as I know," he said, "they have various timing beams, but that happens wherever we test and race. Knowing how quickly a car is going doesn't mean you know how it does it."

14 July *Alesi to stay with Prost*
French driver Jean Alesi has said that he will stay with Prost next season, despite the many difficulties that the team has encountered this year. Alesi's decision appears to be based chiefly on his personal regard for team boss Alain Prost. "It feels good to work with Alain," Alesi said, "and I would like to stay with him as long as I can."

eaders, "best of the rest" fight for scraps

Right: Jenson Button, a surprise choice by Williams at the start of the season, has performed better than most observers predicted.

Far right: Sir Frank Williams has ensured that his team make good use of the extra power provided by their new BMW engine.

Above: Mika Salo demonstrates the speed that has given Sauber a measure of success this season.

Left: Alex Wurz has fallen far short of his Benetton team-mate Fisichella in performance.

BAR, who entered Formula One with absurd expectations of instant success in 1999, scraped into middle-ranking status in the first half of 2000 – due largely to the driving skills of Jacques Villeneuve. To justify the vast cash-input from their sponsors they needed further progress by the season's end.

Jaguar were playing the same role as BAR in 1999 – achieving minimal results for vast investment. Grafting new personnel on to the old Stewart team had clearly not worked, and the car was unreliable and difficult to drive. Given Ford's huge commitment to Jaguar, something had to improve.

Small but beautiful

Sauber and Arrows showed potential both in their cars and their drivers. Sauber's Mika Salo revealed again what a fine racer he is, while Arrows' Pedro de la Rosa was impressive. But these teams had no more realistic chance of being title contenders than did the hapless Prost and Minardi.

Austrian Grand Prix

The Circuit

The A-1 Ring was built during the winter of 1995–96 to replace the Österreichring track. Like its popular predecessor, the A1-Ring encourages exhilarating, high-speed racing, its sweeping corners providing some excellent opportunities for cars and drivers to demonstrate their qualities. On the minus side, overtaking can be difficult on this circuit.

Track length 4.319 km (2.684 miles)
Race distance 306.640 km (190.543 miles) — 71 laps
1999 winner Eddie Irvine, Ferrari
Lap record 1:11.814 min, Jacques Villeneuve, Williams-Renault, 1997

Race Result

	Driver	Time
1	Hakkinen	1:28:15.818
2	Coulthard	1:28:28.353
3	Barrichello	1:28:46.613
4	Villeneuve	1 lap behind
5	Button	1 lap behind
6	Salo	1 lap behind

Drivers' Championship

	Driver	Points
1	M. Schumacher	56
2	Coulthard	50
3	Hakkinen	48
4	Barrichello	36
5	Fisichella	18
6	R. Schumacher	14
7	Villeneuve	11
8	Trulli	6
9	Button	5
	=Frentzen	5

Salo, 4 points. Irvine, 3 points. Verstappen, 2 points. De la Rosa, Zonta, 1 point.

Constructors' Championship

	Constructor	Points
1	Ferrari	92
2	McLaren	88*
3	Williams	19
4	Benetton	18
5	BAR	12
6	Jordan	11

Sauber, 4 points. Arrows, Jaguar, 3 points.
*After 10 points were deducted for an infringement of technical regulations.

Mika Hakkinen was in command throughout the race weekend, dominating the qualifying session as well as the race itself.

The reigning champion **Mika Hakkinen** returned to **winning form** after Ferrari's Michael **Schumacher** had made an **enforced exit** in a first-corner crash.

Mika tells Michael "It isn't over yet"

The world champion is back – that was the clear message from the Austrian Grand Prix. Observers who had written off Mika Hakkinen as a spent force were made to eat their words. The Finn drove faultlessly from start to finish. Instead, it was Michael Schumacher whose title hopes began to falter as both McLaren drivers closed the points gap.

Qualification

Michael Schumacher looked a worried man after the qualifying session, and with good reason. He had been outpaced not only by the two McLarens, but also by team-mate Rubens Barrichello. Fourth place on the grid is not where Schumacher expects to find himself.

Finn on form

David Coulthard again looked quick and confident, but it was the return to form of Mika Hakkinen that will have set alarm bells ringing in the Ferrari camp. After a rest from testing prescribed by team boss Ron Dennis, the Finn seemed restored to mental fitness, taking the 26th pole position of his career.

It was a good session for BAR, and especially for Ricardo Zonta. The Brazilian for once qualified ahead of team-mate Jacques Villeneuve, although he was beaten for fifth place by Jarno Trulli.

Jaguar performed poorly after losing their lead driver at the last moment, when Eddie Irvine was hospitalized with suspected appendicitis. Williams had no such excuse for their worst qualifying performance of the year.

Qualifying Times

1	Hakkinen	McLaren	1:10.410
2	Coulthard	McLaren	1:10.795
3	Barrichello	Ferrari	1:10.844
4	M. Schumacher	Ferrari	1:11.046
5	Trulli	Jordan	1:11.640
6	Zonta	BAR	1:11.647
7	Villeneuve	BAR	1:11.649
8	Fisichella	Benetton	1:11.658
9	Salo	Sauber	1:11.761
10	Verstappen	Arrows	1:11.905
11	Diniz	Sauber	1:11.931
12	De la Rosa	Arrows	1:11.978
13	Heidfeld	Prost	1:12.037
14	Wurz	Benetton	1:12.038
15	Frentzen	Jordan	1:12.043
16	Herbert	Jaguar	1:12.238
17	Alesi	Prost	1:12.304
18	Button	Williams	1:12.337
19	R. Schumacher	Williams	1:12.347
20	Gené	Minardi	1:12.722
21	Burti	Jaguar	1:12.822
22	Mazzacane	Minardi	1:13.419

Schumacher's race lasted only seconds. Both he and Barrichello made a slow start, so Zonta and Trulli, on the third rank of the grid, were right under the Ferraris' rear wings going into the first corner. A fraction late in braking, Zonta hit Schumacher's car, sending it into a spin. Schumacher in turn hit Trulli, who had already nudged Barrichello. The Ferrari number two was able to continue, albeit with a damaged car, but Schumacher and Trulli were out of the race.

Schuey shrugs it off

Schumacher was surprisingly philosophical about the incident, considering its impact on his title prospects. The worst he would say about Zonta was that he had been "over-enthusiastic". The McLaren team were less courteous about Schumacher, accusing him of nursing his car back on to the tarmac after the accident in a deliberate effort to have the race stopped and restarted.

Schumacher was, in fact, not the only driver who thought a restart would have been appropriate.

Fisichella was also a victim of the mayhem at the first corner, hit from behind by Pedro Diniz. After the race the Benetton driver said: "I can't believe that there wasn't a red flag."

But, in the event, the safety car was deployed and the race continued. The chief beneficiaries were, of course, the two McLarens, but some other drivers found themselves

Above: Hit by Ricardo Zonta, Schumacher spins off. Main image: After the race Hakkinen's joy is unconfined.

promoted well above their positions on the grid. These included Salo, Herbert, Button, and De la Rosa, who ran impressively in third place for almost half the race until gearbox trouble ended a brilliant drive.

Despite the damage to his car, Barrichello battled back to fourth place, elevated to third when De la Rosa retired, but never mounted any

threat to the McLarens. Hakkinen powered into a 15-second lead over Coulthard by lap 30, which the Scot never attempted to challenge.

Behind the leaders, Villeneuve once more showed his exceptional driving skills. He lost out in the first-corner chaos, but forced his way back up through the field, and pulled off a quick late pit-stop to move into fourth

place. Behind him Button, Salo, and Herbert scrapped for fifth place. Despite an excursion off the track on lap 53, the Williams driver won this contest, with Salo deservedly taking the last points position.

There was no question that the day belonged to Hakkinen. The Finn claimed that, as well as benefitting from a rest, he had taken advantage of

Schumacher was unhappy with the decision to let the race continue.

a new set-up which had restored the car to his liking. "We've solved the problems we had and I'm back to what I used to be," Hakkinen said. Referring to the race for the drivers' title, he added: "It's not over yet."

Missing seal

A shadow was cast over McLaren's triumph after the race, with the news that the FIA had found a paper seal missing on the electronic control unit of Hakkinen's car. McLaren issued a statement saying they were confident that Hakkinen's victory would be allowed to stand. All but the most rabid Ferrari fans agreed that he deserved 10 points for a faultless drive.

Mixed fortunes for Jaguar's rookie substitute driver

Jaguar's Brazilian test driver Luciano Burti was thrown into the F1 crucible at short notice when Eddie Irvine withdrew on the Friday before the race weekend. Under the circumstances, Burti put on a creditable show. He qualified 21st, but was only 0.6 seconds adrift of Johnny Herbert. In the race itself, a mechanical problem on the grid meant he had to change to Herbert's spare car and start from the pit-lane. But this helped him avoid the first-corner chaos, a stroke of luck that promoted him to 12th position. Burti said, "After that it was just a matter of concentrating." He finished 11th.

Luciano Burti in the pits during his unexpected grand prix debut.

BETWEEN THE RACES

25 July *McLaren pay penalty as Hakkinen keeps points*

Following the revelation that the seal on the electronic control unit (ECU) of Mika Hakkinen's McLaren was missing after the Austrian Grand Prix, an FIA meeting in London has decided to take 10 constructors' championship points away from the McLaren team, but allow Hakkinen to keep the drivers' championship points for his victory. The stewards agreed that the team could not have used illegal software and Hakkinen could not have gained any unfair advantage. McLaren were, however, guilty of an infringement of technical regulations.

17 July *Franchitti tests with Jaguar Racing*

The Scottish Champ Car star Dario Franchitti has begun two days of testing with the Jaguar Racing team at Silverstone. Runner-up to Juan Pablo Montoya in last year's CART championship, Franchitti drove for Paul Stewart Racing before moving to America and has maintained links with many personnel in the new Jaguar team. Jaguar boss Neil Ressler is obviously interested in Franchitti as a possible team-mate for Eddie Irvine in the 2001 season. Some observers believe that Ressler would prefer to sign up Giancarlo Fisichella, but it is unlikely that Benetton would be prepared to release the impressive Italian driver to a direct competitor.

The Arrows cars will be powered by a Peugeot-derived engine next season.

20 July *New Arrows engine deal as Peugeot pull out of F1*

Long-standing rumours that Peugeot were to leave Formula One at the end of the season have been confirmed today. The former Peugeot engine programme is to be taken over by Asia Motor Technologies (AMT). Peugeot's move will end the motor company's unhappy relationship with the Prost team, which will now have to look for a new engine supplier. AMT will continue to develop the Peugeot engine and will supply Arrows in 2001. Arrows previously had a deal with Supertec costing $20 million a year. It is assumed that the Peugeot-derived engines supplied by AMT will be considerably cheaper.

21 July *Car giants to buy in to Formula One*

The ever-growing interest of motor manufacturers in Formula One has been confirmed by news that major firms, said to include Toyota, Ford, Fiat, and BMW, are negotiating to buy a substantial stake in Bernie Ecclestone's SLEC Holdings, as well as in German media group EM.TV, which recently bought half of SLEC. Apart from giving another massive injection of capital to the already cash-rich Formula One scene, the involvement of industrial giants looks set to limit the influence of individual team owners. It could also see all F1 teams tied to an engine supplier, with no more shopping around for engines.

24 July *Villeneuve opts for three more years at BAR*

After weeks of speculation suggesting that Jacques Villeneuve would sign for Benetton-Renault, the former world champion has decided instead to stay with BAR. He has agreed a three-year contract said to be worth $50 million. Recent improvements in performance and reliability apparently convinced the Canadian driver that BAR could offer the prospect of a championship challenge. Benetton-Renault are said now to have made an approach to Jenson Button, who is not wanted by Williams next year.

Johnny Herbert will soon be on his way to America after a long F1 career.

26 July *Herbert to quit Formula One at season's end*

British driver Johnny Herbert has confirmed that he will leave Jaguar at the end of the season to seek a new racing career in America. Although a three-times grand prix winner in a Formula One career stretching back more than a decade, Herbert has never achieved the success that seemed to be within his grasp. His decision to leave Formula One comes as no surprise. At a press conference in Frankfurt, Herbert said: "I have decided that I will go to the American CART series next year. Obviously, I've still got to sign a contract for a drive, but that is what I want to do next year."

Champ Car driver Dario Franchitti is being lined up as a possible driver for Jaguar.

Is enigmatic Jacques losing his way?

WITHIN FORMULA ONE THREE men compete for the accolade of top driver: Michael Schumacher, Mika Hakkinen – and Jacques Villeneuve. Yet, since he won the world drivers' championship while at Williams in 1997, Villeneuve has rarely had the opportunity to show even brief flashes of the brilliance that makes him one of the motor-racing elite.

Many experienced observers feel that, by agreeing to sign on with BAR for another three years rather than joining the Benetton-Renault team, the French-Canadian driver has now denied himself the best chance he could have had to fulfil his outstanding potential.

The non-conformist

Yet it is his refusal to live by others' rules that makes Jacques Villeneuve interesting as a man and driver. The current world of Formula One places a premium on conformity. Drivers, like other personnel, are subordinate to the needs of the team. But Villeneuve is an individualist who cares little for convention – so much so that, were his skills less superb, he would be unemployable as a driver in Formula One. Indeed, there are still those who would be happy to pass Villeneuve over in favour of more pliable individuals, real team players who, for example, dutifully accept their tedious PR duties as a necessary part of an F1 driver's job.

Living for thrills

Like all good racers Villeneuve takes risks, but whereas most drivers will accept risk as a means to an end, for Villeneuve risk is an end in itself, off the track as well as on. He continues to ski, and by his own admission takes as many chances on the slopes as he does when racing. And one of his few PR stunts this year was to hurl a sponsor-blazoned powerboat around the harbour at Monte Carlo.

Lost in the rough: Jacques Villeneuve walks away from yet another BAR mechanical failure, ending his part in the 2000 Brazilian Grand Prix.

Arguably the biggest risk taken by Villeneuve was leaving Williams for BAR in 1998. The $15 million a year he reputedly earns can be no hardship, but the real key to his decision to join BAR, and stay there, must lie in his close relationship with team principal Craig Pollock.

Pollock – who originally taught Villeneuve at a Swiss school – has occupied a crucial role in his former pupil's life. Villeneuve asked him to become his personal manager while racing in Japan in 1992, and Pollock has continued to fill that position up to the present day. Armchair psychologists might argue that Pollock fulfils some sort of father-figure role for Villeneuve, but whatever the reason he is one of the few people to have a hold on the French-Canadian maverick.

Pollock has nailed his colours to the mast of BAR, a gamble that the risk-taking Villeneuve has seen fit to follow. The two men will now either sink together, or sail on to triumph over their sceptical critics.

Early triumphs: Villeneuve as IndyCar champion in 1995 (above) and as Formula One world champion two years later (above right).

30 JULY • HOCKENHEIM
German Grand Prix

A **bizarre** grand prix, interrupted by an **intruder on the track,** brought an **emotional first victory** for Rubens Barrichello – from **18th place** on the grid.

The Circuit

The Hockenheim Ring is one of the longest grand prix circuits. In the main it comprises a series of fast straights and corners through dense forest, but there is a slower stadium complex of tight corners before the finishing line. Setting up cars for both of these contrasting track sections is difficult because the downforce that is needed for the tight bends also slows the cars on the straights. The weather at Hockenheim is often changeable, if not downright wet.

Track length 6.822 km (4.239 miles)
Race distance 307.305 km (190.755 miles) – 45 laps
1999 winner Eddie Irvine, Ferrari
Lap record 1:45.270 min, David Coulthard, McLaren-Mercedes, 1999

Every driver who wins a grand prix for the first time enjoys the experience, but there was something extra special in Rubens Barrichello's heartfelt joy after his unlikely victory.

Race Result

	Driver	Time
1	Barrichello	1:25.34.418
2	Hakkinen	1:25.41.870
3	Coulthard	1:25.55.586
4	Button	1:25.57.103
5	Salo	1:26.01.530
6	De la Rosa	1:26.03.497

Drivers' Championship

	Driver	Points
1	M. Schumacher	56
2	Coulthard	54
	=Hakkinen	54
4	Barrichello	46
5	Fisichella	18
6	R. Schumacher	14
7	Villeneuve	11
8	Button	8
9	Salo	6
	=Trulli	6

Frentzen, 5 points. Irvine, 3 points. De la Rosa, Verstappen, 2 points. Zonta, 1 point.

Constructors' Championship

	Constructor	Points
1	Ferrari	102
2	McLaren	98
3	Williams	22
4	Benetton	18
5	BAR	12
6	Jordan	11

Sauber, 6 points. Arrows, 4 points. Jaguar, 3 points.

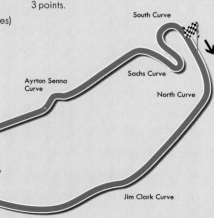

South Curve

Sachs Curve

North Curve

Ayrton Senna Curve

East Curve

Jim Clark Curve

Rubens to the rescue for Ferrari

Qualification

Four minutes into a rain-affected qualifying session at Hockenheim, David Coulthard laid down a flying lap which was 1.4 seconds better than any of his rivals was to manage throughout the entire 60 minutes.

Scrap for second

In between rain showers, Benetton's Giancarlo Fisichella grabbed a provisional second place, but he was subsequently relegated to third after a superb lap by Michael Schumacher in the final moments, which earned the German a place on the front row next to Coulthard. Mika Hakkinen could only manage fourth, while the third row of the grid was filled by the surprisingly fast Arrows of Pedro de la Rosa and by Jarno Trulli's Jordan.

Brazilian nightmare

The biggest loser of the session was Rubens Barrichello. His Ferrari broke down on his first flying lap and he was forced to use the spare T-car, which was then being run by Schumacher. For a long period the Brazilian failed to set a qualifying time, but during the last five minutes he managed to scrape home as a miserable 18th on the grid.

Qualifying Times

1	Coulthard	McLaren	1:45.697
2	M. Schumacher	Ferrari	1:47.063
3	Fisichella	Benetton	1:47.130
4	Hakkinen	McLaren	1:47.162
5	De la Rosa	Arrows	1:47.786
6	Trulli	Jordan	1:47.833
7	Wurz	Benetton	1:48.037
8	Herbert	Jaguar	1:48.078
9	Villeneuve	BAR	1:48.121
10	Irvine	Jaguar	1:48.305
11	Verstappen	Arrows	1:48.321
12	Zonta	BAR	1:48.665
13	Heidfeld	Prost	1:48.690
14	R. Schumacher	Williams	1:48.841
15	Salo	Sauber	1:49.204
16	Button	Williams	1:49.215
17	Frentzen	Jordan	1:49.280
18	Barrichello	Ferrari	1:49.544
19	Diniz	Sauber	1:49.936
20	Alesi	Prost	1:50.289
21	Mazzacane	Minardi	1:51.611
22	Gené	Minardi	1:53.094

The German Grand Prix at Hockenheim was the stage for one of the most eventful races in recent Formula One history. It included spins, multiple crashes, rain storms, safety cars, and a protester wandering around on the track. But it will above all be remembered for Brazilian Rubens Barrichello's first grand prix victory, at the 124th attempt.

Above: Even the McLaren drivers join the celebrations after Barrichello's victory. Above right: Frustration for Schumacher as he is hit from behind by Giancarlo Fisichella – the German's second first-corner exit in a fortnight.

Mika Hakkinen, fourth on the grid, made a lightning getaway, threading between Coulthard and Schumacher to take the lead by the first corner. Coulthard, by contrast, had a poor start and swerved across Schumacher's path to take the inside line. Blocked by Coulthard, Schumacher went over to the outside and in so doing drove in front of Fisichella. With nowhere to go, the Benetton driver clipped the rear of Schumacher's Ferrari, causing both cars to crash out of the race.

The Ferrari camp were facing disaster: for the third time in a row Schumacher had failed to finish, while their other driver had started from 18th place on the grid. As

Hakkinen and Coulthard raced away into the distance, a McLaren one-two seemed to be the likeliest prospect.

Intruder on the track

On lap 24, a figure was seen walking across and alongside the track. The safety car soon came out as security staff apprehended the man, a former Mercedes employee protesting against his dismissal by the company.

The incident had unfortunate consequences for Coulthard, for while most drivers nipped in for a pit-stop,

the Scot stayed out and was stuck behind the safety car. As a result, after he did make his refuelling stop he found himself in sixth place.

The safety car reemerged on lap 29 after a spectacular crash between Alesi and Diniz. But more influential for the course of the race was the onset of rain, falling heavily on parts of the track, but less so on others.

Barrichello, who was running on a lighter, two-stop fuel load, had carved his way through the field during the early laps, and by the time

Fisichella unrepentant over Schumacher shunt

Giancarlo Fisichella, the target for Schumacher's anger.

After the clash of cars came the clash of words, as Michael Schumacher and Giancarlo Fisichella argued about their coming together at the first corner.

Schumacher refused to blame Coulthard for blocking him. "It was nothing to do with David," he said. "I lost my race because of Fisichella. I was hit from behind by Fisichella — he should have been more careful."

Fisichella, however, put the blame firmly on Schumacher. "He cut across me and took my line," he said. "I was on my line and suddenly Michael's car was in front of my front wheel."

the first drops of rain began to fall had advanced to third place. While most other drivers decided to come in for wets, the Brazilian held out on the track, so moving into the lead.

Gambling on dries

Coulthard also decided to stay out, taking second place, until a near spin made him also dive in for wets. But

Barrichello persisted with dry tyres. Over the radio, Ferrari technical director Ross Brawn told him: "If you can keep to the lap times you're running now, Rubens, you'll win." Brawn's assessment proved correct. The wet-dry track enabled Barrichello to hold his position against any attack from his pursuers, Hakkinen and Coulthard, in the final stages.

Jean Alesi was lucky to walk away unscathed after a collision with Pedro Diniz's Sauber.

Barrichello's was not the only fine drive of the day. Button started from the back of the grid after stalling before the formation lap. But, after the rain began, he charged through the field to seize fourth place. And Jarno Trulli was in second position when an unfortunate stop-go penalty took him out of the reckoning for points.

But the race belonged to Barrichello. One of the best-liked drivers in Formula One, he was greeted with affectionate acclaim for his first grand prix victory. Tears streamed down his face as he stood on the podium. It had been an emotional day.

Invasion o`

BETWEEN THE RACES

Ricardo Zonta driving for BAR — a sight possibly unlikely to be seen next season.

1 August *Coulthard adopts new driving tactics*

David Coulthard has admitted that he deliberately swerved across the track in order to avoid being overtaken by Michael Schumacher's Ferrari at the start of the German Grand Prix. Having been the victim of similar moves from Schumacher in the past, Coulthard said that such tactics were now a part of Formula One racing and open to all to use as they saw fit. Describing the incident — which ended with Schumacher colliding with Fisichella's Benetton — Coulthard said: "I just got too much wheelspin, and I knew I was making a bad start from the moment that I went off the line. So I

just wanted to try and make it as difficult as we are allowed for someone to pass me." Schumacher, for his part, refused to condemn Coulthard's manoeuvre, reserving his ire solely for Fisichella.

2 August *Villeneuve damns team-mate Zonta*

BAR driver Jacques Villeneuve has torn into team-mate Ricardo Zonta following a coming together which saw both drivers spin out of the German Grand Prix on lap 34. "Since the start of the season," Villeneuve fumed, "I haven't told the media that I have very little respect for Zonta. Now I can say it: I have no respect for him at all." He continued: "As long as Zonta stays behind me, as is the case the majority of the time, it doesn't bother me, but he wanted to be a hero by overtaking me."

In reply, Zonta said: "I am very sorry for what happened to Jacques. He made a small mistake on the last corner, and I had the opportunity to overtake him. He gave me space, but not quite enough, and I touched the kerb as a result. It was slippery and the car slid out a little and my front wheel clipped his rear wheel."

3 August *Salo tempted by Toyota*

Sauber driver Mika Salo has admitted that he has seriously considered an offer to join Toyota for the 2001 season. The Toyota deal would entail testing during 2001, before the company enters Formula One in 2002. Although Salo has

said he is happy at Sauber, a long-term contract with Toyota appeals to the 32-year-old driver: "I am not a young boy any more and the Toyota offer stretches well beyond my racing career, so I have to think carefully about it," he said.

Mika Salo ponders a move to Toyota.

4 August *Valencia test crashes*

Alexander Wurz has been injured in a crash during a testing session at Valencia. The Benetton driver ended up in hospital after a front suspension wishbone went through the cockpit tub and penetrated his leg, an injury similar to that suffered by Ralf Schumacher at the Monaco Grand Prix. The injury is not considered serious enough to stop him from racing in the Hungarian GP. David Coulthard also came off the track in a high-speed shunt, spinning round five times in the gravel trap. He emerged from his car unhurt.

5 August *Real Thing to sponsor F1*

The soft-drink giant Coca-Cola is set to enter Formula One as a major team sponsor. The American company had previously shown little interest in motor sport, but the global appeal of Formula One has convinced Coca-Cola that it could be a profitable advertising vehicle. Formula One is keen to involve such a major corporation, especially as it is looking for new sponsorship sources to reduce its traditional dependence on revenues from tobacco advertising.

David Coulthard reflects on his chances of the championship.

he Champ Cars is planned for next year

THE US CART SERIES IS COMING TO Europe for the 2001 season. Two races will be held — at the Lausitzring in eastern Germany on 15 September, and a week later at Rockingham in Northamptonshire. A classic Champ Car oval is currently being built for the occasion at the English venue.

CART racing already occurs at support venues outside its traditional American base — in South America, Mexico, Canada, Japan, and Australia. But the decision to go into Europe is a gamble, part of a conscious attempt to revitalize Champ Cars. Declining attendance figures over the last few years, exacerbated by a recent feud with the competing IRL series, are causing serious concern to the teams and organizers of CART. In a recent shake-up former champion driver and current team owner Bobby Rahal has taken over as CART president. He has given his firm support to the introduction of oval racing in Europe.

Critical comparisons

Whether the two races in Europe will have any effect on Formula One is a matter of conjecture. The simpler but more powerful Champ Cars are considerably faster than their Formula One counterparts, and when driving on oval circuits overtaking is not merely possible but is a common occurrence. Although lacking the sophistication of the highly regulated F1 vehicles, Champ Cars provide the sort of wheel-to-wheel excitement that is often lacking in Formula One.

However, BAR boss Craig Pollock, who managed Jacques Villeneuve in CART for two seasons before coming over to Formula One, welcomed the move. "There is no reason why it won't be a great success," he said. "It is a good spectacle and should draw the crowds. There is room for F1, and there is room for Champ Cars."

In search of a public

Pollock is almost certainly right that these two variants of motorsport can happily coexist, but whether the CART races will be able to attract enough fans is harder to assess.

There is a large British contingent in Champ Cars — both drivers and constructors — which should help matters at Rockingham. But whether the Schuey faithful can be persuaded to change "codes" and drive east to Lausitzring looks more doubtful. Mercedes motorsport boss Norbert Haug is sceptical: "I cannot see it being a success at all," he said. "It will be difficult to attract 100,000 people there." Only time will tell.

Above left: A typical CART oval with banked corners, designed for speed. Above right: CART stars Juan Pablo Montoya and Michael Andretti fight it out wheel-to wheel. Left: A CART oval in Japan.

13 AUGUST • HUNGARORING
Hungarian Grand Prix

The Circuit

Built in 1986 especially for grand prix racing, the Hungaroring is a relatively slow, bumpy, and slippery track. A good starting position and careful pit and race strategy tend to win races — overtaking is notoriously difficult. The circuit is traditionally regarded as a home venue for Finnish drivers, whose national supporters travel to Hungary in their thousands for the grand prix.

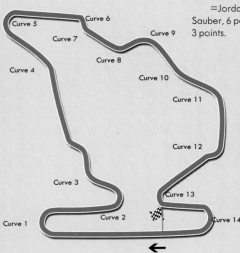

Race Result

	Driver	Time
1	Hakkinen	1:45.33.869
2	M. Schumacher	1:45.41.785
3	Coulthard	1:45.42.324
4	Barrichello	1:46.18.026
5	R. Schumacher	1:46.24.306
6	Frentzen	1:46.41.968

Drivers' Championship

	Driver	Points
1	Hakkinen	64
2	M. Schumacher	62
3	Coulthard	58
4	Barrichello	49
5	Fisichella	18
6	R. Schumacher	16
7	Villeneuve	11
8	Button	8

Frentzen, Salo, Trulli, 6 points. Irvine, 3 points. De la Rosa, Verstappen, 2 points. Zonta, 1 point.

Constructors' Championship

	Constructor	Points
1	McLaren	112
2	Ferrari	111
3	Williams	24
4	Benetton	18
5	BAR	12
	=Jordan	12

Sauber, 6 points. Arrows, 4 points. Jaguar, 3 points.

Track length 3.968 km (2.465 miles)
Race distance 305.536 km (189.805 miles) — 77 laps
1999 winner Mika Hakkinen, McLaren
Lap record 1:18:308 min, Nigel Mansell, Williams-Renault, 1992

McLaren team boss Ron Dennis congratulates Mika Hakkinen, who is visibly drained by his energy-sapping winning drive.

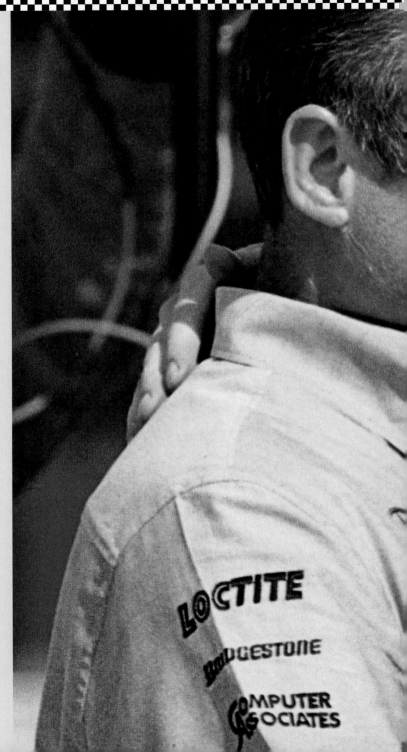

The **McLaren revival** continued as Mika **Hakkinen** displayed absolute **dominance** in a race in which heat and **dehydration** were harder to beat than **Ferrari**.

Second-best Schumacher is shaken by dominant

Qualification

Given that overtaking is so difficult in Hungary, Ferrari worked hard to produce a car that could get their main driver pole position. Michael Schumacher waited until halfway through the session before emerging from the pits; he then set the fastest time of the afternoon at his first attempt. Ferrari's decision to use scrubbed front tyres and new rears, an unconventional strategy, worked well, and Schumacher was nearly four-tenths of a second clear of his nearest rival.

McLarens in pursuit

David Coulthard complained of understeer caused by running a low fuel-load, but his last run put him alongside Schumacher on the front row. Fellow McLaren driver Mika Hakkinen was unhappy with the set-up of his car throughout the session and had to be content with third.

Rubens relegated

After his triumph in Germany, Rubens Barrichello came down to earth with a bump, as a much-improved Ralf Schumacher pushed past him to secure fourth. The Brazilian was relegated to a position on the third row of the grid alongside the Jordan of Heinz-Harald Frentzen.

Qualifying Times

1	M. Schumacher	Ferrari	1:17.514
2	Coulthard	McLaren	1:17.886
3	Hakkinen	McLaren	1:17.922
4	R. Schumacher	Williams	1:18.321
5	Barrichello	Ferrari	1:18.330
6	Frentzen	Jordan	1:18.523
7	Fisichella	Benetton	1:18.607
8	Button	Williams	1:18.699
9	Salo	Sauber	1:18.748
10	Irvine	Jaguar	1:19.008
11	Wurz	Benetton	1:19.259
12	Trulli	Jordan	1:19.266
13	Diniz	Sauber	1:19.451
14	Alesi	Prost	1:19.626
15	De la Rosa	Arrows	1:19.897
16	Villeneuve	BAR	1:19.937
17	Herbert	Jaguar	1:19.956
18	Zonta	BAR	1:20.272
19	Heidfeld	Prost	1:20.481
20	Verstappen	Arrows	1:20.609
21	Gené	Minardi	1:20.654
22	Mazzacane	Minardi	1:20.905

Mika Hakkinen seemed to draw strength from the mass of blue and white flags waved from the stands by the Finnish fans who had flocked to Hungary for the race weekend. He recorded an emphatic victory and, for the first time this season, pushed Michael Schumacher off the top of the championship table. The balance of power was swinging away from Schumacher to Hakkinen, and from Ferrari to McLaren.

Mika Hakkinen owed his victory to a blistering start from third place on the grid, which propelled him past Coulthard and Schumacher and into the lead by the first corner. Michael Schumacher could not keep up, and even though the difference was only a few tenths of a second a lap, it was sufficient to underscore the clear superiority of McLaren over Ferrari.

Clearly shaken by Hakkinen's performance, Schumacher had few answers. "If we continue like this," he

Hakkinen nips past Schumacher at the first corner — the decisive moment in an otherwise uneventful race.

said, "we have no chance. Even if I had kept the lead, Mika would probably have overtaken me at a pit-stop." Ferrari technical director Ross Brawn explained that the main problem lay in the inability of Schumacher to maintain consistent grip with his tyres: if he pushed hard for a lap, grip would be reduced,

Hakkinen

forcing him to ease up. But why the McLaren should have better grip with the same tyres baffled the Ferrari team. Afterwards, Brawn said: "We'll have to go back and think again. No stone will be left unturned."

Traditional procession

Once the start was over, the race settled down to the predictable procession that is the Hungarian Grand Prix. After shaking off an early challenge from Ralf Schumacher,

Coulthard suffered from balance problems during the early stages of the race that prevented him from closing on Schumacher senior. After the first round of stops the Scot clearly had the edge over Schumacher, but he was unable to get past the Ferrari.

Coulthard's only hope lay in the second round of stops, but his inability to cut through traffic cost him dear. Clearly frustrated by a day that further dented his title chances, the Scot said: "A couple of times I was

held up unnecessarily by the Minardis and when I came out after my final stop behind Michael I had no chance."

Exhausting victory

Mika Hakkinen emerged exhausted from his car after a long drive in intense heat. "I feel like I have been in a two-hour boxing match, and I was the one taking all the punches," he said. It later emerged that, because of a problem with his drinks bottle during the second half of the race, he

Schumacher called for "chassis developments" to make his Ferrari competitive – throwing the problem into the lap of company president Luca Di Montezemolo (inset).

had suffered from severe dehydration and consequent painful cramps.

But the real pain was being felt by Ferrari. Schumacher made it plain that he needed the company to come up with a more competitive chassis if he was going to deliver the goods.

BETWEEN THE RACES

Bernie Ecclestone is cuddly with the McLaren and Ferrari drivers at the Hungaroring, but he shows a distinctly less amiable attitude to journalists who pry into his business affairs.

17 August *Button joins Benetton*

Young British driver Jenson Button will join the Benetton team next season on a two-year loan from Williams, who have Button under contract until the end of 2004. The driver told journalists: "I felt that Benetton offered me the best opportunity of doing what I want to do above all else – to win races." Williams are to replace Button with CART star Juan Pablo Montoya, a decision that some commentators feel the team may come to regret.

17 August *AMT to begin engine testing soon*

Asian Motor Technologies, which recently bought out Peugeot's F1 engine facility, are due to begin work on the 2000-spec Peugeot A21 engine in October. Contracted to supply the Arrows team with engines for next season, AMT intend to fit an A21 engine into an Arrows car for a testing session in Barcelona.

19 August *Bridgestone build a new tyre for US Grand Prix*

As a result of fears that the partially banked Indianapolis GP circuit would pose tyre-wear problems, Bridgestone have constructed a special tyre for the event. Teams believed conventional tyres would not be able to cope with the very different requirements of the ultra-fast banked curves and the twisty infield section. The new tyre has been specially strengthened, sufficient, say Bridgestone, to cope with Indianapolis conditions.

Their confidence is shared by BAR designer Malcolm Oastler, who has had previous experience in CART series racing. "We go through curves like that at other [F1] circuits," said Oastler, "but without the banking. The banking has the effect of adding quite a bit of vertical g-load that transfers to the tyres. But it is something we have done before, and we know the tyres can take it."

22 August *Ecclestone biography probes business deals*

Journalist Terry Lovell is reportedly attempting to find a publisher for a biography of Formula One supremo Bernie Ecclestone which probes deeply into the Ecclestone business empire.

The book apparently talks about Ecclestone's offshore bank accounts and his attempted million-pound donation to Tony Blair's New Labour. Lovell may well have a struggle to publish his controversial account, however, as Ecclestone is known for his defensiveness about his private business affairs.

24 August *Telefonica will continue to underwrite Minardi*

The huge Spanish telecommunications conglomerate Telefonica has announced that it will continue to finance Formula One's smallest team. Throughout much of the season, rumours have circulated that Minardi might be taken over by Telefonica and re-sited away from Italy to Spain, but a spokesman for the company said that their prime concern was to sponsor Spanish driver Marc Gené as part of the Minardi team. The influx of Telefonica cash has helped ensure the retention of top technical director Gustav Brunner and the acquisition of Supertec engines. The determination of Telefonica to ensure a high Spanish profile may encourage Minardi to consider signing Spanish F3000 hopeful Fernando Alonso to drive for them next season.

26 August *Newey not going to the Scuderia*

The ongoing rumour that McLaren aerodynamics guru Adrian Newey might be moving to Ferrari has been denied by both teams. A report in the Italian press suggested that Newey was bound for Maranello – as an eventual replacement for present designer Rory Byrne – on a three-year contract worth a breathtaking $24 million. But Ferrari sporting director Jean Todt denied any such involvement, suggesting that such talk was merely an attempt to destabilize the team. Newey, however, admitted that an offer from Ferrari would have its appeal: "Everybody in F1 dreams about working in Maranello at some time," he declared. "If Ferrari made an offer, I would certainly think about it."

Marc Gené is crucial to Telefonica's support for F1 minnows Minardi – the Spanish company wants a Spanish driver to back.

The alliance between speed and smoke

A PROFITABLE LIAISON BETWEEN Formula One racing and the tobacco industry began in 1968. As a result of growing health concerns, tobacco companies had started to lose many of their existing advertising outlets, above all television, and as a way of circumventing these restrictions they moved into the sponsorship of sport. Formula One was able to offer what the tobacco companies' advertising agencies wanted – a sport with a wide international coverage and projecting a unique aura of glamour.

From the 1970s onwards cars began to resemble flying cigarette packets, while cash from the tobacco firms fuelled the rapid expansion of Formula One from a cottage industry into the technological and financial monster it has become today.

Through the 1990s, however, the cosy relationship between tobacco and Formula One came under increasing threat. The European Union publicly committed itself to ending all forms of tobacco advertising. The FIA fought back with all its considerable might, and in a series of bitter battles held off a proposed EU tobacco ban. Formula One also expanded its operations in Asia and the Far East, which were key expanding markets for Western tobacco companies.

Living without nicotine

In 2000, however, the World Health Organization announced that it was drawing up a treaty banning all tobacco sponsorship on a global basis. The proposed convention, which is likely to be legally binding, is set to come into force in 2003 or 2004.

The consequences of such a ban for the funding of Formula One will be momentous. Although there has been a decline in tobacco advertising in the sport over the last few years, its role is still sizeable. Williams, in the past allied to Rothmans, Camel, and Winfield, have now moved towards technology and computer companies such as Compaq for sponsorship. But many teams are still closely identified with the tobacco industry. They include McLaren, Ferrari, Jordan, Benetton, Prost, and, especially, BAR.

Pulling the plug

British American Tobacco (BAT) is the chief shareholder in BAR, with a holding recently increased to at least 85 per cent. If Formula One becomes a tobacco-free zone then BAT will presumably pull out. This puts BAR's long-term survival in some doubt.

Altogether, the outlook for the future relationship between smoking and Formula One does not look promising. It has been a long and largely happy affair, but breaking up is likely to prove messy and painful.

Above: "Flying cigarette packet" cars of the 1970s and 1980s – the Lotus JPS, Marlboro McLaren, and Lotus Camel. Left: Prost still have tobacco sponsorship, but alongside new-technology sponsors.

27 AUGUST • SPA

Belgian Grand Prix

Spa-Francorchamps

The Circuit

Following the route of an old country road through the wooded hills of the Ardennes, the Spa-Francorchamps circuit is the longest in F1. Interestingly combining high- and low-speed sections, the course includes a very fast bend at Blanchimont and the fast and demanding downhill bend at Eau Rouge.

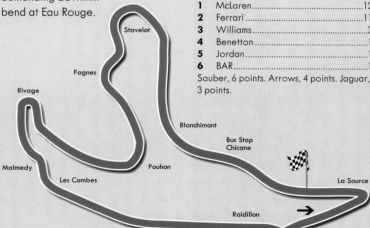

Stavelot

Fagnes

Rivage

Blanchimont

Bus Stop Chicane

Malmedy

Pouhon

Les Combes

La Source

Raidillon

Kemmel

Eau Rouge

Track length 6.968 km (4.330 miles)
Race distance 306.597 km (190.516 miles) — 44 laps
1999 winner David Coulthard, McLaren
Lap record 1:51.095 min, Alain Prost, Williams-Renault, 1993

Race Result

	Driver	Time
1	Hakkinen	1:28.14.494
2	M. Schumacher	1:28.15.597
3	R. Schumacher	1:28.52.590
4	Coulthard	1:28.57.774
5	Button	1:29.04.408
6	Frentzen	1:29.10.478

Drivers' Championship

	Driver	Points
1	Hakkinen	74
2	M. Schumacher	68
3	Coulthard	61
4	Barrichello	49
5	R. Schumacher	20
6	Fisichella	18
7	Villeneuve	11
8	Button	10
9	Frentzen	7

Salo, Trulli, 6 points. Irvine, 3 points. De la Rosa, Verstappen, 2 points. Zonta, 1 point.

Constructors' Championship

	Constructor	Points
1	McLaren	125
2	Ferrari	117
3	Williams	30
4	Benetton	18
5	Jordan	13
6	BAR	12

Sauber, 6 points. Arrows, 4 points. Jaguar, 3 points.

Mika Hakkinen has recovered the will to win and set his sights on a third consecutive drivers' title.

Despite **spinning off** early in the race, Hakkinen surged past **Michael Schumacher** in a memorable **overtaking manoeuvre** to grab maximum points.

Schumacher overtaken in Mika masterclass

Qualification

Mika Hakkinen and his McLaren MP4/15 dominated the session, a near perfect combination of man and machine ensuring a pole-position time that was nearly eight-tenths faster than anyone else.

Small sensation

A fast qualifying session from Hakkinen was no surprise, but the times of Jarno Trulli and new boy Jenson Button caused a minor sensation as they took second and third places respectively. Button's placing must have been particularly encouraging as it put him well ahead of his experienced team-mate Ralf Schumacher, qualifying for sixth place on the grid.

Breaking ranks

The Jordan and the Williams broke up the old order of scarlet and silver, with Michael Schumacher having to accept fourth and David Coulthard demoted to fifth. The Scot said he had suffered from problems of tyre grip, although his best run was thwarted by Frentzen's Jordan, and words were exchanged between the two drivers after qualifying. Rubens Barrichello had an even worse session — he could only manage a miserable 10th.

Qualifying Times

1	Hakkinen	McLaren	1:50.646
2	Trulli	Jordan	1:51.419
3	Button	Williams	1:51.444
4	M. Schumacher	Ferrari	1:51.552
5	Coulthard	McLaren	1:51.587
6	R. Schumacher	Williams	1:51.743
7	Villeneuve	BAR	1:51.799
8	Frentzen	Jordan	1:51.926
9	Herbert	Jaguar	1:52.242
10	Barrichello	Ferrari	1:52.444
11	Fisichella	Benetton	1:52.756
12	Irvine	Jaguar	1:52.885
13	Zonta	BAR	1:53.002
14	Heidfeld	Prost	1:53.193
15	Diniz	Sauber	1:53.211
16	De la Rosa	Arrows	1:53.237
17	Alesi	Prost	1:53.309
18	Salo	Sauber	1:53.357
19	Wurz	Benetton	1:53.403
20	Verstappen	Arrows	1:53.912
21	Gené	Minardi	1:54.680
22	Mazzacane	Minardi	1:54.784

Even if Ron Dennis slightly over-egged Mika Hakkinen's 41st-lap overtaking move on Michael Schumacher by calling it the "best manoeuvre ever", Hakkinen did prove that he was more than just a fine driver in a superb car. After this race he could justifiably assume the title of a great racer, a man prepared to push beyond calculated risk — someone who could be compared with the likes of Mansell and Senna.

As so often in the past, storm clouds gathered over Spa and heavy rain fell over much of the track before the race started. Fearful of any repetition of the mayhem of the rain-swept 1998 Belgian Grand Prix, the authorities ordered a rolling start behind the safety car. This controversial move denied spectators the traditional excitement of the mad dash for La Source, but at least the race got under way without incident. There was one early accident when a heavily loaded Trulli was knocked out of the race by an over-enthusiastic Button.

The pre-race rainfall left the track an uncertain mix of wet and dry. From lap 6 onwards the drivers made their decision to go on to dry tyres, and began to dive into the pits. As at

Hockenheim, Coulthard's hopes of a good finish were dashed by his team's delay in bringing him into the pits, which left him stuck behind Frentzen's Jordan for much of the race.

McLaren mishap

As the circuit dried, the front runners Hakkinen and Schumacher began to carve out a lead, the McLaren proving a little too fast for the Ferrari. But Schumacher's moment came when Hakkinen spun after skidding over a

Hakkinen (top) sets the pace, while Ferrari fans (above) watch their team struggling to keep up.

wet kerb. The McLaren stayed on track, but the spin allowed the Ferrari to fly past. After this incident the race looked to be going Schumacher's way. Hakkinen had the edge in speed, but the Ferrari blocked the McLaren at every passing opportunity.

With only four laps left to go, however, Schumacher moved to the

Left: Hakkinen has every reason to feel elated after a victory that owed as much to his skill and nerve as to the superiority of the McLaren car.

left to overtake backmarker Ricardo Zonta. Rather than take the usual route of following Schumacher to pass Zonta, Hakkinen made the split-second decision to overtake the BAR on the right. Despite being on the wet part of the track, the Finn gained sufficient tow to get past both Zonta and Schumacher in one deft move.

It was a breathtaking manoeuvre which was as daring as it was skilful. From then on the outcome of the race was largely a formality. Schumacher was generous in defeat. "It was a superb move," he said. "Usually there is only room for two cars abreast on the track at that point, but Mika made an outstanding pass." But, admitting the current superior speed of the McLarens, Schumacher also said that Hakkinen was bound to pass him some time.

Button (above right) reflects on a flawed race after sensational qualifying, while Barrichello (below right) knows that his title challenge is over.

Below: Ralf Schumacher on his way to his second podium place of the season – an impressive drive on an excellent race weekend for Williams.

Behind the leaders, Ralf Schumacher drove another sound race, his third place reflecting the improvement in the BMW-Williams. After losing places as a result of the Trulli encounter, Jenson Button came in fifth, adding to a combined Williams total that comfortably extended the team's third place lead over Benetton. But the gap between the top two and the rest remained as wide as ever.

BETWEEN THE RACES

29 August *Trulli forgives Button*

Although clearly annoyed at the time, Jordan's Jarno Trulli has subsequently adopted a philosophical attitude to his clash with Jenson Button during the opening stages of the Belgian Grand Prix. Button tried to squeeze past Trulli at La Source, but he clipped the Jordan, spinning it out of the race. "You have to be professional when you are driving with everyone else," said Trulli, "and you have to accept that someone else made a mistake. I wasn't very happy, but I couldn't show everybody my feelings right after the accident because you need to be calm, or you will say things that you regret."

30 August *Stormy scenes at F1 summit*

At a tense meeting in a hotel at Heathrow airport, outside London, FIA President Max Mosley has confronted team bosses dissatisfied at the way the sport is being run. Led by Ron Dennis, Eddie Jordan, and Sir Frank Williams, the team chiefs were apparently critical of the FIA's role within Formula One and called for Mosley to stand down as president or, at least, not to seek re-election in October 2001.

The exchanges at the meeting are believed to have become particularly heated when it was suggested that the FIA manipulated the rules in an effort

Two drivers *who came together at Spa: a touch from Jenson Button (top) put Jarno Trulli out of the race after the Jordan driver had started from the front row of the grid.*

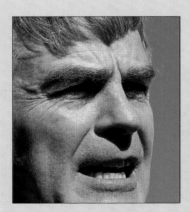

Max Mosley *was on the defensive after coming under fire from prominent F1 team bosses.*

to ensure that the championship went down to the last race, and also that it was biassed in favour of Ferrari.

Mosley's position as FIA president is not dependent on the Formula One teams but on the votes of various international motoring organizations, a point Mosley made clear to the meeting. Afterwards, he told the press: "It is no business of the teams who the president is. It would be like me saying that Ron Dennis should resign as head of McLaren. All they can do is choose whether or not they want to enter this championship."

During the seven-hour meeting, a variety of other topics came under discussion, including the need to improve Formula One as a spectator sport. The role of the Friday race sessions was debated, with suggestions ranging from introducing combined Friday-Saturday qualifying to abandoning Friday sessions altogether.

The teams' continuing disenchantment with extensive testing between races was discussed, and it seems likely that limitations will come into force in the near future. More controversial was the difficult question of rule interpretation,

particularly in regard to electronics. The FIA prefers general guidelines which it can interpret at will, while the teams want stricter written rules.

30 August *Silverstone HQ for Jaguar*

Jaguar has unveiled plans for its new headquarters, which are to be built alongside the Silverstone GP circuit. The new headquarters — which will cost at least $100 million — will group the Cosworth engine team with the main chassis construction facility, alongside a state-of-the-art wind tunnel — an essential part of any successful F1 operation. The British Racing Drivers' Club, which owns Silverstone, will benefit significantly from an influx of funds from Ford.

4 September *Suspend racing in August, says Jordan*

Speaking at Jordan's 10th anniversary celebrations at Donington, team boss Eddie Jordan called for a mid-season suspension of the racing calendar. Jordan noted that the grand prix season placed heavy demands on the teams and their staffs, which, he believed, would increase over time. Jordan said: "I think there will be a blanket ban for the month of August, and I hope there will be. I think summer is a time for families to spend together, otherwise we will chase away high-quality personnel into other areas of the industry."

7 September *Monza chicane changes worry drivers*

In advance of the Italian Grand Prix, several leading Formula One drivers have expressed concern at changes made to Monza's Variante Goodyear and Variante della Roggia chicanes, intended to slow drivers and deter them from kerb-hopping. Although Ferrari driver Michael Schumacher expressed his approval of the modifications, other drivers felt that they would force the cars to slow and bunch-up more than before, increasing the risk of accidents.

F1 teams line up their drivers for 2001

SETTLING WHICH DRIVERS ARE moving and which staying put for the following season took a long time this year, mostly because of the long-drawn-out fan dance between Jacques Villeneuve and Benetton – would he go or would he stay? Villeneuve's decision to stay with BAR eventually freed the market log-jam.

Button on loan

Williams had made it clear that they wanted CART sensation Juan Pablo Montoya, which meant that Jenson Button had to leave. Now that Villeneuve was no longer moving to Benetton, the way was open for team boss Flavio Briatore to take the young English driver on a two-year loan, to partner Giancarlo Fisichella.

The loan deal put Williams in a win-win situation: if Button failed to cut the mustard their decision to let him go would be vindicated; if he was a success at Benetton, Williams would be able to bring him back to the team as a fully-fledged F1 driver.

Jordan followed the lead of F1 top dogs McLaren and Ferrari in keeping their driver line-up intact, although there were rumours that Jaguar wanted Heinz-Harald Frentzen as part of their effort to spearhead car sales into Germany. This was only one example of how, in the famously cosmopolitan world of Formula One, sponsorship continued to exert a nationalist influence. Prost's backers wanted a French driver and were satisfied by the re-signing of Jean Alesi; and Sauber cast a favourable eye over Alex Wurz, no longer wanted at Benetton, because Red Bull, one of their main sponsors, were Austrian.

Swiss swap

Sauber were set to lose both their drivers: Mika Salo signed a contract with Japanese manufacturer Toyota, while Pedro Diniz was ready to swap places with Prost's Nick Heidfeld.

By contrast, Arrows decided to hold on to both their drivers, Tom Walkinshaw's team evidently pleased by the spirited performances of Jos Verstappen and Pedro de la Rosa.

Two test drivers have made their mark. Jaguar's Luciano Burti is set to

Top: Fisichella accepts Briatore's offer of another year at Benetton. Above: Jaguar boss Ressler (right) introduces driver Burti to the press.

replace a tired Johnny Herbert. And Olivier Panis, who spent the season as a test driver for McLaren after a miserable year at Prost in 1999, has worked his passage back into F1. A seat alongside Villeneuve at BAR shows that a spell out of racing does not mean professional suicide.

This might be of comfort to two of the losers in this year's round of musical chairs. Ricardo Zonta, excess to requirements at BAR, has been touted to replace Panis as test driver at McLaren, who are also keen to secure the services of a second ex-F1 driver. This could mean a place for Wurz if he does not take up the Sauber option. In the world of Formula One, what goes around tends to come around.

Former world champion Jacques Villeneuve's decision to stay at BAR left a free seat at Benetton for Jenson Button.

10 SEPTEMBER • MONZA
Italian Grand Prix

An **emotional** Michael Schumacher was **in tears** after a victory that **delighted the tifosi** but was marred by the tragic **death** of a fire marshal in a **first-lap pile-up.**

The Circuit

The Italian Grand Prix was first held at the Autodromo Nazionale di Monza in 1950. Monza is the fastest circuit in Formula One, in spite of its many chicanes. Engine power is very important. Drivers maximize their speed on the long straights by operating with very little wing, but the price is reduced ground adhesion on the slower sections of the circuit.

Track length 5.769 km (3.585 miles)
Race distance 305.757 km
(190.005 miles) — 53 laps
1999 winner Heinz-Harald Frentzen, Jordan
Lap record 1:24.808 min, Mika Hakkinen, McLaren-Mercedes, 1997

Race Result

	Driver	Time
1	M. Schumacher	1:27.31.638
2	Hakkinen	1:27.35.448
3	R. Schumacher	1:28.24.070
4	Verstappen	1:28.31.576
5	Wurz	1:28.39.064
6	Zonta	1:28.40.930

Drivers' Championship

	Driver	Points
1	Hakkinen	80
2	M. Schumacher	78
3	Coulthard	61
4	Barrichello	49
5	R. Schumacher	24
6	Fisichella	18
7	Villeneuve	11
8	Button	10

Frentzen, 7 points. Salo, Trulli, 6 points. Verstappen, 5 points. Irvine, 3 points. De la Rosa, Wurz, Zonta, 2 points.

Constructors' Championship

	Constructor	Points
1	Mclaren	131
2	Ferrari	127
3	Williams	34
4	Benetton	20
5	BAR	13
=	Jordan	13

Arrows, 7 points. Sauber, 6 points. Jaguar, 3 points.

Ferrari fans' favourite sight: Michael Schumacher on his way to victory.

Day of joy, frustration, and tragedy at Monza

Qualification

On-going technical improvements and recent driving knowledge of the revised Monza circuit clearly worked to Ferrari's advantage in the qualifying session, with Michael Schumacher and Rubens Barrichello claiming both positions on the front row of the grid. Barrichello was racing to his full potential – the Brazilian only missed taking pole position as a result of the awkward presence of Heinz-Harald Frentzen's Jordan on his flying lap.

McLarens divided

Hakkinen and Coulthard could only manage third and fifth respectively, while Villeneuve's BAR – using a new Honda qualifying engine – divided the two McLaren drivers. Coulthard was unlucky in again being balked by Frentzen, who seemed to be driving without mirrors in Italy, as he had in Belgium two weeks before.

The less powerful BMW engines of the Williams cars struggled to make an impact on the Monza power circuit, although Ralf Schumacher was able to take some consolation from a reasonable seventh spot, where he found himself sandwiched between the Jordans of Trulli and Frentzen.

Qualifying Times

1	M. Schumacher	Ferrari	1:23.770
2	Barrichello	Ferrari	1:23.797
3	Hakkinen	McLaren	1:23.967
4	Villeneuve	BAR	1:24.238
5	Coulthard	McLaren	1:24.290
6	Trulli	Jordan	1:24.477
7	R. Schumacher	Williams	1:24.516
8	Frentzen	Jordan	1:24.766
9	Fisichella	Benetton	1:24.789
10	De la Rosa	Arrows	1:24.814
11	Verstappen	Arrows	1:24.820
12	Button	Williams	1:24.907
13	Wurz	Benetton	1:25.150
14	Irvine	Jaguar	1:25.251
15	Salo	Sauber	1:25.322
16	Diniz	Sauber	1:25.324
17	Zonta	BAR	1:25.337
18	Herbert	Jaguar	1:25.388
19	Alesi	Prost	1:25.556
20	Heidfeld	Prost	1:25.625
21	Gené	Minardi	1:26.336
22	Mazzacane	Minardi	1:27.360

The death of a track-side fire marshal cast a deep shadow over what would otherwise have been a perfect result for Michael Schumacher. Ferrari at last managed to stem the tide of recent McLaren victories, ensuring that the fight for the title would continue on the other side of the Atlantic. But the fatality – the first in Formula One since Senna's death at Imola in 1994 – underlined the dangers inherent in the sport.

The accident that led to the death of fire marshal Paolo Ghislimberti occurred on the first lap at the second chicane. The field was still bunched up, braking hard from over 180 mph, when Frentzen ran into Trulli and Barrichello, sending all three cars spinning down the track and into a gravel trap. In a cloud of dust, they collected up Coulthard's McLaren, with gravel, wheels, and various car parts all flying through the air.

Death of a marshal

The ensuing chaos caused De la Rosa's Arrows to cannon off the Jaguar of Johnny Herbert and then somersault through the air before coming to a halt on the side of Barrichello's Ferrari. Miraculously, none of the drivers was hurt, but part of a disintegrating car fatally wounded the fire marshal, who died shortly afterwards in hospital.

Despite the seriousness of the accident, which left carbon-fibre debris scattered across the track, the race was surprisingly not red-flagged. The safety car cruised around for the next 11 laps as the circuit was cleaned up. But as the safety car prepared to return to the pit lane further drama ensued: unexpected hard braking by Schumacher caught many of the leading cars by surprise, sending

Above: His title chances ended by the crash, David Coulthard reflects on a season of wasted opportunity.

sixth-placed Jenson Button off the track and out of contention.

After the long-delayed departure of the safety car, the race was largely uneventful. Schumacher's Ferrari always had the edge over Hakkinen's

Left: Fraternal celebrations for the Schumacher brothers, first and third.

McLaren, possessing superior speed and grip. Such excitement as there was came from the contest for the lesser points positions.

Continuing his good run of form Ralf Schumacher achieved another podium finish. The earlier culling of much of the field opened the way for the Arrows of Jos Verstappen to cross the line fourth, while the next two places went, ironically, to drivers who had lost their seats for next season, Alexander Wurz and Ricardo Zonta.

Record victory

That Schumacher's victory at Monza was his 41st, equalling the record of the great Ayrton Senna, was not lost on Schumacher himself, or the capacity 125,000 crowd. At a highly wrought press conference, held before news of the fatality had reached the drivers, the normally ice-cool German broke down with emotion.

When asked why the victory meant so much to him, Schumacher eventually replied: "It's obvious: we are here in Italy. The crowd outside has been amazing. We were in some difficulty in the last races where we weren't as competitive as we wished, but now we are back on the road."

The unfortunate Coulthard had other emotions, as he was forced sadly to admit that his title chances were over. "I've just got to do my best in the last few races," the Scottish driver said, "and then try again next year."

Schumacher or Hakkinen – the championship was down to a straight fight, and looked likely to go to the final race.

Above: On the first lap, Frentzen (centre) runs into Trulli and Barrichello at the second chicane; Coulthard, in front of the Jordans, was caught up in the crash a split second later. Left: De la Rosa's Arrows somersaults off the track. Below: Barrichello climbs out of his car as officials run to the aid of De la Rosa, who landed upside down alongside the Ferrari.

BETWEEN THE RACES

Monza: Is i

12 September *Modifications to Formula One year*

Following a meeting between Formula One teams and the FIA at Monza, a number of new proposals to change the working of the sport have been accepted. Chief amongst these is a reduction in the amount of testing conducted throughout the year. It was agreed that only four circuits should be used for testing – Barcelona, Magny-Cours, Silverstone, and Monza. No testing will be allowed at any circuit in the four weeks leading up to a grand prix being held there.

This ruling is partly intended to encourage teams to make fuller use of the Friday practice sessions. Another boost for Friday practice is an increase in the tyre allowance for a race weekend from eight to ten sets.

The teams and the FIA also agreed that there should be a three-week break in the racing calendar during August. This measure will come into effect in the 2001 season.

13 September *Frentzen answers his critics after Monza disaster*

Following the fatal first-lap accident at Monza, Jordan's Heinz-Harald Frentzen has replied to criticisms levelled at him by Rubens Barrichello.

Immediately after the incident, a furious Barrichello claimed that Frentzen was the culprit and said that he should be banned for ten grand prixs. In response, Frentzen gave a description of the accident from his own point of view. "I had made a good start," he explained, "and was up to sixth place. I was then slipstreaming Barrichello near the middle of the track as we came through the Curva Grande. When Rubens braked he did so earlier than I had expected. It took me by surprise. I simply could not stop my car in time, and I hit the back of Ruben's rear wheel with my front wing. As I automatically reacted by moving to the right in order to avoid the Ferrari, my team-mate Jarno Trulli suddenly appeared ahead, and I couldn't avoid him either."

Frentzen blamed the crash on the Monza chicanes: "When you have cars bunched up at over 300 km/h (180 mph)," he said, "all of them braking for a slow chicane, accidents are sometimes inevitable."

Frentzen was exonerated by the race stewards after they reviewed the video evidence of the accident.

20 September *CART boss Rahal to become Jaguar team principal*

At a press conference in Indianapolis, where F1 teams have arrived for the United States Grand Prix, Jaguar chairman Neil Ressler announced that

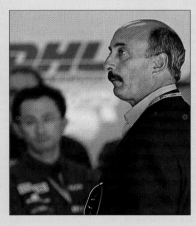

Bobby Rahal meets the Jaguar team that he is going to lead into next season.

Heinz-Harald Frentzen denies being at fault in the fatal first-lap crash at Monza.

Bobby Rahal, a former Champ Car champion and current CART president, is to become the new team principal of Jaguar Racing. He will take up the post at the start of December.

Rahal has worked with Ressler in the past, after Team Rahal became a Ford works team in the CART series. He will move to Britain to oversee the troubled Jaguar team, which he believes can be one of the best in Formula One. "Success won't come overnight," he said, "but I believe it is attainable. There are a lot of capable people at Jaguar. I don't think that it's as bad as it looks."

21 September *Prost to receive Ferrari engines next season*

Prost's increasingly desperate search to find an engine supplier has ended with the news that Ferrari are ready to supply engines to the French team in a two-year deal. Prost therefore join Sauber as a Ferrari engine customer. Speaking with renewed optimism after the setbacks of the last six months, Alain Prost said that the new powerplant would provide the team with a high level of reliability and competitiveness for next season.

THE ACCIDENT THAT LED TO THE death of a fire marshal at this year's Italian Grand Prix has produced calls for new safety measures and revisions to the circuit at Monza.

Chicanes have been the focus of most criticism. They were introduced at Monza in 1972 as a safety device, slowing cars down on the fastest track in Formula One. But they were also directly responsible for the bunching up of cars that caused the accident.

After the race, Formula One boss Bernie Ecclestone condemned the chicanes as "silly and unnecessary".

really safe enough?

He called for them to be replaced by single, slow-speed corners. Max Mosley, the FIA president, said that parts of the Monza circuit might have to be redesigned, but denied that the Italian Grand Prix was under threat.

Drivers protected

The fact that no drivers were hurt in the mass pile-up proved that recent rule changes to improve driver safety have worked well. But less attention has been paid to the safety of race marshals. Several drivers noted that some of the marshals were not even stationed behind the barriers but were standing exposed in vulnerable track-side positions.

The death may have been caused by a wheel from Frentzen's car. The inability of a single steel cable to tether a wheel to a car in a violent accident has long been a safety problem. Next season two cables will be fitted per wheel, which should make flying wheels less of a danger.

One of the controversial chicanes at Monza, which are regarded by some drivers as a serious safety hazard.

Names to watch for in the future of F1

Above: Promising young French F3000 driver Nicolas Minassian.

FORMULA ONE IS ARGUABLY THE hardest of all sporting clubs to enter. The competition for the 22 drivers places is intense. At the end of every season there is usually a maximum of two or three places open to the best of the potential newcomers. So who are the possible Jenson Buttons of 2001?

Raw talent

To get noticed at all, a young driver needs to have raw talent and racing experience in one of the junior racing formulas, such as Formula 3000 or Formula 3. In 2000 the man to watch has been 23-year-old Brazilian Bruno Junqueira. He seemed to be lined up for a Formula One seat at Williams early in the year, but Button was surprisingly chosen in his place. Junqueira bounced back to win the Formula 3000 championship, and his evident skills have now attracted the attention of a number of Formula One and CART series teams.

Budding stars

Other stars from F3000 who may have a future at the top in Formula One include the French runner-up in this year's competition, Nicolas Minassian; Australian driver Mark Webber, who is a likely test driver with Benetton next season; and the young Spanish

Above: This year's F3000 champion, Brazilian driver Bruno Junqueira.

driver Fernando Alfonso, who is thought to have an option to drive one of the Spanish-funded Minardis.

Among current F3 racers, Tomas Scheckter (the son of the former F1 world champion Jody Scheckter), Antonio Pizzonia, and Takuma Sato all look good prospects, while Kimi Raikkonen, the British Formula Renault champion, has impressed Sauber at test sessions. They all know that fame and fortune could be theirs — or simply fail to materialize.

24 SEPTEMBER • INDIANAPOLIS
US Grand Prix

The largest crowd in Formula One history witnessed the return of F1 to the United States, and the return of Schumacher to the lead in the world title contest.

The Circuit

The new Formula One circuit at the Indianapolis Motor Speedway was created by welding a twisty infield section on to the existing IndyCar oval. The result is a circuit with a long main straight, led in to by a fast banked turn, but also with tight hairpins. The downforce needed to negotiate the infield prevents the cars being set up to exploit the full speed potential of the main straight.

Track length 4.194 km (2.605 miles)
Race distance 306.200 km
(190.165 miles) — 73 laps
Lap record 1:14.711 min, David Coulthard, McLaren-Mercedes, 2000

Race Result

	Driver	Time
1	M. Schumacher	1:36.30.883
2	Barrichello	1:36.43.001
3	Frentzen	1:36.48.251
4	Villeneuve	1:36.48.819
5	Coulthard	1:36.59.695
6	Zonta	1:37.22.577

Drivers' Championship

	Driver	Points
1	M. Schumacher	88
2	Hakkinen	80
3	Coulthard	63
4	Barrichello	55
5	R. Schumacher	24
6	Fisichella	18
7	Villeneuve	14
8	Frentzen	11
9	Button	10
10	Salo	6
	=Trulli	6

Verstappen, 5 points. Irvine, Zonta, 3 points.
De la Rosa, Wurz, 2 points.

Constructors' Championship

	Constructor	Points
1	Ferrari	143
2	McLaren	133
3	Williams	34
4	Benetton	20
5	BAR	17
	=Jordan	17
7	Arrows	7

Sauber, 6 points. Jaguar, 3 points.

F1 is back: the cars go into the first corner at a packed Indianapolis.

Mika's championship lead goes up in smoke

Qualification

A new grand prix circuit produced no surprises at the front of the grid, where the top four places were once again shared between the Ferrari and McLaren drivers.

Ferrari in tow

One novelty, however, was the use of slip-streaming by both teams. On the long straight Barrichello gave Schumacher a valuable tow for a flying lap that brought the German pole position. McLaren copied the Ferrari tactic towards the end of the session. As Hakkinen had only an in-and-out lap, it was Coulthard who was given the tow. The Scottish driver came close, but could not beat Schumacher's time. Hakkinen was relegated to the second row alongside Barrichello, not the best position from which to challenge for a first-corner lead.

On the button

Jenson Button's fine qualifying run continued – he took sixth place alongside Jarno Trulli, while his team-mate Ralf Schumacher could only manage tenth place. Button's successor at Williams, Juan Pablo Montoya – in Indianapolis as a guest of the team – was no doubt left with plenty of food for thought.

Qualifying Times

1	M. Schumacher	Ferrari	1:14.266
2	Coulthard	McLaren	1:14.392
3	Hakkinen	McLaren	1:14.428
4	Barrichello	Ferrari	1:14.600
5	Trulli	Jordan	1:15.006
6	Button	Williams	1:15.017
7	Frentzen	Jordan	1:15.067
8	Villeneuve	BAR	1:15.317
9	Diniz	Sauber	1:15.418
10	R. Schumacher	Williams	1:15.484
11	Wurz	Benetton	1:15.702
12	Zonta	BAR	1:15.784
13	Verstappen	Arrows	1:15.808
14	Salo	Sauber	1:15.881
15	Fisichella	Benetton	1:15.907
16	Heidfeld	Prost	1:16.060
17	Irvine	Jaguar	1:16.098
18	De la Rosa	Arrows	1:16.143
19	Herbert	Jaguar	1:16.226
20	Alesi	Prost	1:16.471
21	Mazzacane	Minardi	1:16.609
22	Gené	Minardi	1:17.161

In front of a 220,000-strong crowd, Ferrari won a crucial one-two victory at Indianapolis. The flames that licked around Mika Hakkinen's engine at the end of lap 26 dealt a grievous – perhaps mortal – blow to his chances of winning a third consecutive title. Hakkinen's justified gloom was countered by the euphoria of Michael Schumacher and Ferrari. Schuey clearly had the scent of victory in his nostrils.

Top: Coulthard (front left) jumps the start. Above: Schumacher attacks and finds a way past Coulthard, with Hakkinen hovering in the background.

McLaren's misfortunes began from the start, when David Coulthard's car rolled forward from second place on the grid just before the red lights went out. As a result, Coulthard surged ahead of Schumacher to take the lead, although the McLaren's jump-start meant a certain stop-go penalty. Before the race stewards brought the Scot in to serve his time, he did his best to hold up Schumacher and allow Hakkinen to draw up close behind the Ferrari. But Schuey then passed Coulthard in a fine overtaking manoeuvre using the tow provided by the main Indianapolis straight.

Coulthard immediately let his team-mate through, but Hakkinen was unable to match Schumacher, who began to pull away. When the Finn pitted to exchange his wets for dry tyres, he found himself stuck behind Gaston Mazzacane's Minardi for nearly four laps. Hakkinen was only able to get through when the Minardi eventually went into the pits.

Engine blown

Once past Mazzacane, Hakkinen found his car's true speed and began to reel in Schumacher at the rate of about a second a lap. But when he was only four seconds behind the Ferrari, his engine blew. He limped back into the pits, his race over. Coulthard, in ninth place after serving his stop-go penalty, was only able to fight his way back to fifth before the chequered flag came down on Schumacher.

The latter part of Schumacher's race was so easy that a lapse of concentration caused him to spin the car with only two laps to go. Fortune was with Ferrari: Schumacher quickly regained control and drove to the line, with a radio warning ringing in his ears from Ross Brawn to keep focus.

Relief for Jordan

Behind the leaders, Button had an early clash with Trulli that forced both cars into eventual retirement. Trulli's colleague Frentzen, however, managed his second podium finish of the year, much to the relief of the Jordan team. BAR could also take comfort from their performance, with Villeneuve fourth and Zonta sixth.

After the race Schumacher did his best to play down his prospects. "As for the championship," he said, "I will only believe in it when it is over." But McLaren knew that they needed to raise their game dramatically if they were to have any hope for either the drivers' or constructors' titles.

Above right: A jubilant Schumacher is dowsed by third-placed Frentzen. Right: Hakkinen looks on dejectedly as the fire in his engine is put out.

BETWEEN THE RACES

25 September *US Grand Prix declared a success*

The future of Indianapolis as a grand prix venue seems assured on the basis of comments by leading figures in Formula One. Both Bernie Ecclestone and Max Mosley gave their approval and congratulated circuit owner Tony George on his efforts. Speaking on behalf of the FIA, Mosley said: "The facility is quite remarkable, and I think it will serve as an example to a number of places throughout the world." A record crowd of 220,000 people attended on race day, but some commentators have suggested that this might only reflect curiosity and pre-race hype. The real test of the circuit will come next year.

Max Mosley and Bernie Ecclestone were happy to be back in the US.

29 September *Tomas Scheckter to be the Big Cat's new test driver.*

Following the promotion of Jaguar test driver Luciano Burti to partner Eddie Irvine next season, F3 star Tomas Scheckter is to be the team's new official test driver for 2001. Tomas, the son of 1979 Ferrari world champion Jody Scheckter, impressed Jaguar with his performances in their subsidiary team, Stewart Racing.

2 October *Coulthard OK at US GP, says Schumacher*

Immediately after the grand prix at Indianapolis, Michael Schumacher strongly criticized David Coulthard for allegedly unfair driving that led the two men's cars to touch briefly as Schumacher took the lead on lap 7. But after seeing a replay of the race on video, Schumacher has admitted that his complaints were unfounded. Referring to the incident, Schumacher

said: "In the cockpit, I thought it was over the top, but when I looked at the television footage, it seemed to me that his manoeuvre was quite normal."

3 October *Prost loses Gauloises but finds Stella — and possibly Pedro*

Prost's turbulent year has continued with the announcement that Gauloises are to withdraw as the team's chief sponsor. But this was offset by news that Alain Prost had been in sponsorship talks with the Belgian company Interbrew, the makers of Stella Artois. Meanwhile, speculation continues as to whether Pedro Diniz will become a Prost driver in 2001.

4 October *FIA accepts tobacco ban*

The FIA's World Council, meeting in Seville, has announced that tobacco

Pedro Diniz, driving for Sauber this year, is rumoured to be on his way to Prost.

advertising and sponsorship will cease in Formula One after the 2006 season. The FIA has given in to pressure from the World Health Organization, which is preparing a worldwide ban on the promotion of tobacco products.

5 October *Silverstone back in July*

The finalized 2001 race calendar shows the British Grand Prix returning to its traditional date in mid-July, following a swap with the Austrian Grand Prix. The Australian Grand Prix will once again open the season, on 4 March, while Japan will hold the final race on 14 October. The Malaysian Grand Prix will move back from October to March.

The A-1 Ring will stage the Austrian GP in April after swapping dates with Silverstone.

Is the USA

NO EUROPEAN F1 CIRCUIT CAN boast a pedigree to match that of the Indianapolis Motor Speedway. It has been holding races since 1909 and, as the home of the Indy 500, draws crowds of up to half a million.

Battle of the bricks

The Indianapolis circuit is strong on tradition, and when Ferrari wanted to sandblast the famous yard of bricks at the start-finish line to improve Schumacher's traction for the start of this year's US Grand Prix there were howls of protest. Harmony prevailed when the grid was moved back 17 yards, but the incident revealed some of the potential for misunderstanding that exists in the motor-racing divide between Europe and America.

Chequered history

Technically, Indianapolis has staged numerous US Grand Prixs before, because from 1950 to 1960 the Indy 500 was part of the Formula One

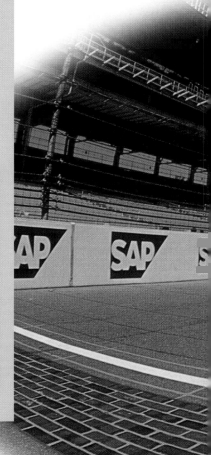

ready to join the world of Formula One?

championship. Few European drivers took part, however, and the available points went to American drivers who did not participate in other F1 races. This bizarre situation typified much of F1's chequered history in America.

The US Grand Prix found a home at Watkins Glen, New York, in the 1960s and 1970s, and from 1976 a second grand prix was successfully introduced at Long Beach, California. In 1982 there were actually three US Grand Prixs – but this was not a sign of progress. Public interest in Formula One faded as various venues were tried out and abandoned – including a Las Vegas car park. The grand prixs held in Phoenix, Arizona, from 1989 to 1991 attracted pitifully little local interest, and the event was dropped.

The massive crowd that paid to see this year's revival at Indianapolis was understandably viewed as a triumph by the organizers, and the circuit seems sure to stage a US Grand Prix for some years ahead. But whether Formula One will become a major attraction in America is still in doubt.

Lukewarm fans

American racing enthusiasts remain lukewarm about Formula One, most considering it too technical and short on thrills and spills. Fans also did not warm to the F1 drivers, who came across as cold and distant – although their main failing may have been that none of them was an American.

Formula One bosses are desperate for success in America because it is the largest market for the sport's sponsors. But it may well be that Formula One needs the United States more than the United States needs Formula One.

Left and far left: US Grand Prixs held in Phoenix, Arizona, from 1989 to 1991 attracted few spectators. Below: The bricks that pave the start-finish line at Indianapolis became a subject of controversy in the different world of Formula One.

8 OCTOBER • SUZUKA
Japanese Grand Prix

Race Result

	Driver	Time
1	M. Schumacher	1:29.53.435
2	Hakkinen	1:29.55.272
3	Coulthard	1:31.03.349
4	Barrichello	1:31.12.625
5	Button	1:31.19.129
6	Villeneuve	1 lap behind

Drivers' Championship

	Driver	Points
1	M. Schumacher	98
2	Hakkinen	86
3	Coulthard	67
4	Barrichello	58
5	R. Schumacher	24
6	Fisichella	18
7	Villeneuve	15
8	Button	12
9	Frentzen	11
10	Salo	6
	=Trulli	6

Verstappen, 5 points. Irvine, Zonta, 3 points.
De la Rosa, Wurz, 2 points.

Constructors' Championship

	Constructor	Points
1	Ferrari	156
2	McLaren	143
3	Williams	36
4	Benetton	20
5	BAR	18
6	Jordan	17
7	Arrows	7

Sauber, 6 points. Jaguar, 3 points.

The Circuit

Originally held at the Fuji Speedway
track, the Japanese Grand Prix has
been staged at Suzuka since 1987.
The Suzuka circuit is unique in F1 in
having a figure-of-eight pattern,
which gives a balance of clockwise
and anti-clockwise driving. It offers
a variety of hilly left and right turns
and is considered to favour the
more experienced drivers who are
familiar with its intricacies.

Track length 5.864 km (3.642 miles)
Race distance 310.772 km (193.026 miles)
— 53 laps
1999 winner Mika Hakkinen, McLaren
Lap record 1:38.942 min, Heinz-Harald
Frentzen, Williams-Renault, 1997

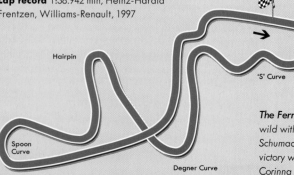

*The Ferrari camp went
wild with joy as Michael
Schumacher celebrated his
victory with his wife
Corinna and the team.*

Michael Schumacher carried off his **third** driver's title and **Ferrari's** first for **21 years** through a **hard-fought** victory over rival **Mika Hakkinen** at Suzuka.

Schumacher upholds his claim to greatness as a

Qualification

As if to underline the gravity of the occasion, the battle for pole was the closest of the year. The two championship contenders gave everything, repeatedly replacing each other as provisional pole leaders until Schumacher laid down a blistering 1:35.825 — an amazing 1.6 seconds faster than the time that gave him pole position in 1999.

Mika's last fling

In the closing minutes of the session Hakkinen went out for a last run to better Schumacher's time. In the first two sectors it looked as if the Finn would do it, but coming out of the final chicane his back end got out of shape, forcing him momentarily to ease off the throttle. He crossed the line just nine thousands of a second behind Schumacher.

Second-row support

The support drivers Coulthard and Barrichello were unable to get near the leaders but comfortably took the second row of the grid. The Williams team did well, taking fifth and sixth places, with Button again out-qualifying his team-mate. Eddie Irvine was able to guide his Jaguar to seventh, just ahead of Heinz-Harald Frentzen's Jordan.

Qualifying Times

1	M. Schumacher	Ferrari	1:35.825
2	Hakkinen	McLaren	1:35.834
3	Coulthard	McLaren	1:36.236
4	Barrichello	Ferrari	1:36.330
5	Button	Williams	1:36.628
6	R. Schumacher	Williams	1:36.788
7	Irvine	Jaguar	1:36.899
8	Frentzen	Jordan	1:37.243
9	Villeneuve	BAR	1:37.267
10	Herbert	Jaguar	1:37.329
11	Wurz	Benetton	1:37.348
12	Fisichella	Benetton	1:37.479
13	De la Rosa	Arrows	1:37.652
14	Verstappen	Arrows	1:37.674
15	Trulli	Jordan	1:37.679
16	Heidfeld	Prost	1:38.141
17	Alesi	Prost	1:38.209
18	Zonta	BAR	1:38.269
19	Salo	Sauber	1:38.490
20	Diniz	Sauber	1:38.576
21	Gené	Minardi	1:39.972
22	Mazzacane	Minardi	1:40.462

Ferrari's campaign to win the F1 world drivers' title with Michael Schumacher had taken five years and reputedly cost the company at least a billion dollars, but for the Maranello faithful it was worth the wait and the money. For Schumacher it was the third title, confirming his place in the pantheon of Formula One greats.

Main picture: The Ferrari sporting director Jean Todt hoists Schumacher into the air during the spectacularly joyous victory celebrations. Right: Schumacher on his way to victory under Suzuka's big wheel.

triple world champion

Ferrari's world championship was very much a team victory. At Suzuka, the brilliance of Ferrari's team-work was exhibited, unsurprisingly, by technical director Ross Brawn, who is the widely acknowledged master of Formula One pit-stop strategy.

Chasing hard

Pole-placed Schumacher lost the lead to Hakkinen at the start. Even though the Ferrari driver attempted to block the Finn, Hakkinen proved too fast and resilient. Schumacher chased hard, however, and was only a couple of seconds behind the McLaren by the time the two drivers went in for their first pit-stops.

Ross Brawn gave Schumacher an extra top-up of fuel, so that when Hakkinen came in for his second pit-stop, the Ferrari driver had a few laps spare in an unladen car to make up the deficit. The weather also came to Michael Schumacher's aid as a light drizzle fell on the track. The Ferrari was better able to cope with the conditions than the McLaren, as Hakkinen explained: "I was sliding all over the track, and I had no grip at all with my new tyres."

Looking good

With only 13 laps left, Schumacher came in for his second stop, which was slightly shorter than Hakkinen's. He then set off down the pit lane with Brawn relating the situation to him over the radio. After the race, the German driver described what happened: "Ross said, 'It's looking good, it's looking good,' and then he said, 'It's looking bloody good!' And then I knew that it was OK. It was the most amazing moment of my career!" Schumacher exited from the pit lane on to the track in the lead, with Hakkinen's McLaren a good four seconds behind him.

From then on, all Schumacher had to do was stay focused and guide

Hakkinen leads Schumacher in the early stages – the two drivers were well clear of the rest of the field.

From the top: Jenson Button puts in another impressive performance to take fifth place; Eddie Irvine has a more encouraging race after a dire season; and Sauber's Pedro Diniz has a fiery time during Saturday morning practice.

his car to the finish line. Hakkinen pressed all the way but he could not get close enough to the Ferrari to mount any challenge.

The Ferrari team's tension in the final stages of the race erupted in an explosion of joy as Schumacher took the race and the world championship. Immediately after climbing out of his car in the parc fermé, the German driver rushed to congratulate every available Ferrari team member, in

recognition of the team's contribution to his personal success. Meanwhile Mika Hakkinen, although clearly downcast, behaved graciously in defeat. "Eventually it is some other driver's turn to win," Hakkinen said, "and to be a good winner you have to be good loser, too. It doesn't mean that you necessarily have to be happy about coming second, but it's good to allow some enjoyment and pleasure for the driver who has won."

BETWEEN THE RACES

Ferrari tifosi celebrate Schumacher's world championship at Maranello.

9 October *Mixed reactions in Italy to Schumacher triumph*

The church bells at Ferrari's home town of Maranello rang out to celebrate Schumacher's victory in Japan, while tens of thousands watching vast television screens in the town square hailed the new world champion. An emotional Ferrari president Luca di Montezemolo, who could not bring himself to travel to Suzuka, said: "We dedicate this title to everyone in Ferrari, and to all those fans around the world who have continued to support us even when things were not going well."

But not everyone in Italy was eager to applaud the new champion. A former Italian president, Francesco Cossiga, was outraged when Schumacher appeared to "conduct" the crowd during the playing of the Italian national anthem. "It annoyed me that an insolent, overpaid Bavarian boy behaves like a good German when he is listening to *Deutschland Uber Alles*," Cossiga fumed, "and then plays the fool — not for the first time — when the Italian national anthem is played."

A diplomatic Schumacher quickly responded to the criticism: "We were all overwhelmed with joy," he said. "I

apologize if my behaviour has been interpreted as a sign of disrespect to Italy's national anthem."

9 October *Jordan confirm Zonta as test driver*

Ending lengthy speculation about his future in Formula One, BAR driver Ricardo Zonta has signed to Jordan to act as their test driver for the 2001 season. Zonta says that he hopes to convince the team that he is worth a race seat for 2002, although this will depend on whether Heinz-Harald Frentzen's contract is renewed at the end of 2001.

10 October *Ralf puts the damper on Montoya mania*

Ralf Schumacher has warned the press not to expect wonders from Juan Pablo Montoya, who will be his new team-mate next season. In the light of Alex Zanardi's problems in transferring from CART to Formula One with Williams in 1999, Schumacher argued for caution: "I am sure Juan will not end up like Alex, but he is obviously putting himself under a lot of pressure by having that reputation and saying what he is saying." Schumacher is known to have wanted Jenson Button to be retained as his team-mate.

11 October *Bridgestone to withdraw from F1 after 2002*

Sources in Japan suggest that Formula One tyre manufacturer Bridgestone intends to pull out of the sport at the end of the 2002 season. Although Bridgestone have not confirmed this rumour, it is thought that the company is generally pulling in its financial horns. Bridgestone are also worried by the potential for adverse publicity in a duel with Michelin in next season's F1 world championship, and they are known to be dissatisfied with grooved tyres, which have no relation to the development of road tyres.

Bridgestone tyres look likely to make their last appearance in F1 in 2002.

12 October *BAR denies Honda buy-out story*

Japanese manufacturer Honda are rumoured to be about to buy out British American Tobacco's majority share in BAR. Honda, who once intended to form their own F1 team, already provide works engines and chassis support to BAR. The BAR management, however, promptly denied that any such move was afoot.

14 October *Schumacher says whispering campaign is unfair*

In an interview with the German press, Michael Schumacher has complained that David Coulthard and Jacques Villeneuve criticize him behind his back. "It's always the same drivers I have problems with, Coulthard and Villeneuve," the new world champion said. "They talk and talk, but they never say anything to my face."

Ralf Schumacher was less than complimentary about Juan Pablo Montoya.

The changing face of F1 for 2001

WHETHER THE 2001 SEASON WILL bring an end to the dominance of Ferrari and McLaren is doubtful. Benetton – with their new Renault tie-up and with driver Jenson Button and designer Mike Gascoyne on board – would like to think they could make an impact, as would Williams, BAR, Jordan, and even Jaguar under new boss Bobby Rahal. But the clever money will be on yet another duel between silver and red for the title.

Tyre wars

Even if the leader board stays much the same, however, there are major changes afoot in the sport. Many fans will be glad to see an end to the Bridgestone tyre monopoly, with the arrival of Michelin in 2001. Even if the Japanese manufacturer's long-term commitment to the sport seems in doubt, next season will at least see some interesting tyre confrontations, an element missing this year.

New safety regulations, including side-intrusion tests, will improve driver safety, and the introduction of double wheel-tethers should prevent the sort of tragedy that marred this season's Italian Grand Prix. Also, restrictions to the rear-wings will cut down on aerodynamic grip, hopefully making overtaking easier.

Left: Eddie Jordan and Jaguar boss Bobby Rahal – the old and new faces of F1. Below: BAR's Craig Pollock, with a make-or-break year ahead.

Potentially the most important new development, however, is the growing long-term intervention of the motor manufacturers in F1. The car makers are not only buying into teams, but are also showing a serious interest in controlling Formula One itself.

Suits in charge

Top manufacturers, including Ford, Renault, FIAT, and BMW, want to buy a major stake in the business that Bernie Ecclestone has built up. The 69-year-old Ecclestone claims he will "run the sport until he is dead", but if the car makers are determined then their money and power are likely to prevail. Swashbuckling team-owners such as Eddie Jordan will have a struggle to survive in a new world of corporate giants and suited executives.

22 OCTOBER • SEPANG
Malaysian Grand Prix

The Circuit

The Sepang circuit, sometimes known as the Shah Alam, staged its first grand prix in 1999 and was immediately voted a success by drivers and spectators alike. No expense was spared in providing facilities that put some other circuits to shame. The only drawback is the likelihood of high temperatures and humidity. The circuit has a wide variation of bends requiring medium downforce settings. The wide track and the long start-finish straight, followed by slow turns, provide overtaking opportunities.

Race Result

	Driver	Time
1	M. Schumacher	1:35.54.235
2	Coulthard	1:35.54.967
3	Barrichello	1:36.13.176
4	Hakkinen	1:36.30.004
5	Villeneuve	1:37.05.427
6	Irvine	1:37.06.803

Drivers' Championship

	Driver	Points
1	M. Schumacher	108
2	Hakkinen	89
3	Coulthard	73
4	Barrichello	62
5	R. Schumacher	24
6	Fisichella	18
7	Villeneuve	17
8	Button	12

Frentzen, 11 points. Salo, Trulli, 6 points. Verstappen, 5 points. Irvine, 4 points. Zonta, 3 points. De la Rosa, Wurz, 2 points.

Constructors' Championship

	Constructor	Points
1	Ferrari	170
2	McLaren	152
3	Williams	36
4	BAR	20
	=Benetton	20
6	Jordan	17

Arrows, 7 points. Sauber, 6 points. Jaguar, 4 points.

Track length 5.542 km (3.444 miles)
Race distance 310.378 km (192.865 miles) — 56 laps
1999 winner Eddie Irvine
Lap record 1:38.540 min, Mika Hakkinen, McLaren-Mercedes, 2000

Under the wigs are Ross Brawn, Schumacher, and Barrichello, celebrating alongside a rueful David Coulthard on the podium.

The **Ferrari victory party** that had started in Japan continued in Malaysia, with **Michael Schumacher** once more **unbeatable**, fighting off his **McLaren rivals**.

Hard-fought contest confirms Ferrari triumph

Qualification

The fearsome strain of fighting for the drivers' championship behind him, Michael Schumacher was in a relaxed mood during qualifying, watching his rivals struggle to set decent times and only leaving the garage during the second half of the session. But Schumacher's relaxed attitude did not extend to the track, and despite limiting his runs he was able to lay down yet another pole position. His time of 1:37.397 was nearly half a second ahead of Mika Hakkinen, who managed to improve narrowly on David Coulthard's best time in the final moments of the session. Rubens Barrichello predictably brought up fourth place.

Wizard Wurz

Of the rest, the best performance was surprisingly that of Alexander Wurz, who gained fifth place, confirming the improvement in his form since he was dropped by Benetton for next year. Villeneuve's BAR had enough power to ensure a third-row placing alongside Wurz. Jaguar could take some comfort from Irvine's hard-fought seventh, just ahead of the Williams of Ralf Schumacher, who, on this occasion, clearly had the edge over Button.

Qualifying Times

1	M. Schumacher	Ferrari	1:37.397
2	Hakkinen	McLaren	1:37.860
3	Coulthard	McLaren	1:37.889
4	Barrichello	Ferrari	1:37.896
5	Wurz	Benetton	1:38.644
6	Villeneuve	BAR	1:38.653
7	Irvine	Jaguar	1:38.696
8	R. Schumacher	Williams	1:38.739
9	Trulli	Jordan	1:38.909
10	Frentzen	Jordan	1:38.988
11	Zonta	BAR	1:39.158
12	Herbert	Jaguar	1:39.331
13	Fisichella	Benetton	1:39.387
14	De la Rosa	Arrows	1:39.443
15	Verstappen	Arrows	1:39.489
16	Button	Williams	1:39.563
17	Salo	Sauber	1:39.591
18	Alesi	Prost	1:40.065
19	Heidfeld	Prost	1:40.148
20	Diniz	Sauber	1:40.521
21	Gené	Minardi	1:40.662
22	Mazzacane	Minardi	1:42.078

As Michael Schumacher crossed the line at Sepang he equalled Nigel Mansell's 1992 record of nine victories in a season. The winning of the constructor's title was icing on the cake for Ferrari, and the entire team, from the caterers to Schumacher himself, donned red wigs to celebrate.

Ferrari's triumph at Sepang summed up much of the season: McLaren fought hard and perhaps could have won through, but the Italian team proved the cooler operators, making the least mistakes to take the prize.

Slow starter

Schumacher's mastery of Formula One has never extended to getting away swiftly at the start, and McLaren hoped to exploit this weakness in the last race of the year. But Hakkinen, acknowledged virtuoso of the fast start, jumped the gun as Coulthard had at Indianapolis. The Finn got away first but the stewards eventually called him in to serve a 10-second stop-go penalty that effectively ruined his chances of victory.

McLaren's hopes then rested on David Coulthard, who had nipped past Schumacher at the first bend and took over the lead from his team-mate Hakkinen just before the penalty stop.

Grassed up

The second McLaren mistake came a few laps later, however. "Unfortunately, I went wide at the start of turn six and picked up some grass which went into the radiator inlets and caused the temperature to rise," Coulthard said. He was called in for an early pit-stop to remove the obstruction and Schumacher swept into the lead, a position that he was able to maintain up to the chequered flag.

Coulthard pressed the champion all the way, but although he had the

Main picture: Schumacher leaps on the podium — wig in pocket. Right: The German driver holds firm under intense pressure from Coulthard.

slightly faster car the advantage was insufficient to let him get past the Ferrari. Hakkinen stormed through the field after serving his penalty, setting a new lap record in the process, but he still crossed the line behind Barrichello, who had followed the leading pair at a respectful distance.

Thrills and spills

Behind the leaders, the field thinned out on the first lap when De la Rosa, Heidfeld, and Diniz departed in a storm of debris. Later in the race Johnny Herbert, appearing for the last time in F1, also crashed out after his rear suspension collapsed while braking at high speed. His team-mate Eddie Irvine, however, achieved Jaguar's second points placing of the season, finishing just behind the impressive Jacques Villeneuve.

Apologies accepted

After the race Coulthard spoke to Schumacher in an effort to defuse a rivalry that had become increasingly bitter during the season. The Scot told the press that he regretted making comments in public that should have been kept private. "I just wanted to apologize to him for that, and say he is a great champion," Coulthard said. Schuey replied that the Scotsman was a "great bloke" – and partied with his red-haired team into the night.

Above left: Hakkinen leads from the start, pulling ahead of Schumacher. Left: De la Rosa and Heidfeld go out of the race spectacularly on lap one.

Magical year for Schuey and Ferrari

AT LAST, ON THE AFTERNOON OF 8 October 2000, Michael Schumacher took the world drivers' title for Ferrari, ending a long and painful 21-year drought for the Italian team. That Ferrari also won the constructors' championship, for the second consecutive year, was almost a side issue, so strong had been the desire for the more coveted of the two titles.

Incomparable triumph

Schumacher had, of course, already won two world championships, with Benetton in 1994 and 1995. But he was emphatic that this year's triumph meant more: "You cannot compare this title with what has gone before," he said. "Ferrari have been without a title for 21 years. There have been so many ups and downs this season, and there were so many points which made it much better than anything that I have had in my life before."

See-saw season

The year started brilliantly for the Scuderia, as Schumacher took the first three races in a row, while main rival McLaren languished among the also-rans. But as the season developed, McLaren fought back, with David Coulthard leading the charge. In mid-season Schumacher faltered, the victim of misfortune and over-zealous driving. Hakkinen then started to assert himself, and the title contest turned into a familiar battle between the top two. Hakkinen's pass of Schumacher at Spa was the high-point of the season, but then engine failure at Indianapolis virtually ended the Finn's hopes of a third successive title.

The Schumacher story

When Schumacher started out in the lower divisions of motor racing, he was seen as a promising driver, but only one of several. He was second to Mika Salo in the European Formula Ford championship in 1988, and equal third with Heinz-Harald Frentzen in the 1989 German F3 series. When he moved to F1 in 1991, however, he was an instant sensation. After a brief stint with Jordan, his move to Benetton in 1992 confirmed him as a champion in the making. In 1996 he joined Ferrari, and the rest, as they say, is history.

Now Schumacher's three world titles place him alongside a select few drivers whose careers are a yardstick against which succeeding generations must be measured. In terms of skill, he can be compared with such legends as Juan Manuel Fangio, Jim Clarke, and Ayrton Senna – although his critics still complain that he has repeatedly crossed the line of bad sportsmanship in his quest for glory.

Future prospects

Now more titles beckon. Willi Weber, Schumacher's manager, is bullish about his client's future prospects: "He is going to stack up a real collection of titles now," Weber said. "This isn't the end, this is the beginning."

Schumacher's contract with Ferrari stretches to the end of 2002, so he has at least a further two seasons with the team. Whether he extends the contract to see out his racing career with the Scuderia probably depends on whether Jean Todt and Ross Brawn decide to stay or go when their contracts run out in 2001.

Team worker

When Schumacher thanks his team for their support he does so genuinely, for one of his greatest strengths is his ability to understand the importance of good team work – especially when it is working for him. But the level of commitment of the Ferrari team was matched by that of Schumacher himself. It was a combination that thoroughly deserved its victory.

Michael Schumacher basks in glory with the Ferrari team, while his closest rival, Mika Hakkinen (inset), has to come to terms with defeat.

DRIVERS' WORLD CHAMPIONSHIP

		Australia	Brazil	San Marino	Britain	Spain	Europe	Monaco	Canada	France	Austria	Germany	Hungary	Belgium	Italy	United States	Japan	Malaysia	Total
1	M. Schumacher	10	10	10	4	2	10	–	10	–	–	–	6	6	10	10	10	10	108
2	Hakkinen	–	–	6	6	10	6	1	3	6	10	6	10	10	6	–	6	3	89
3	Coulthard	–	DQ	4	10	6	4	10	0	10	6	4	4	3	–	2	4	6	73
4	Barrichello	6	–	3	–	4	3	6	6	4	4	10	3	–	–	6	3	4	62
5	R.Schumacher	4	2	–	3	3	–	–	0	2	–	0	2	4	4	–	–	–	24
6	Fisichella	2	6	0	0	0	2	4	–	–	–	–	–	0	0	–	0	0	18
7	Villeneuve	3	–	2	–	–	–	0	0	3	3	0	0	0	–	3	1	2	17
8	Button	–	1	–	2	0	0	–	0	0	2	3	0	2	–	–	2	–	12
9	Frentzen	–	4	–	0	1	–	0	–	0	–	–	1	1	–	4	–	–	11
10	Trulli	–	3	0	1	0	–	–	1	1	–	0	0	–	–	–	0	0	6
=	Salo	DQ	–	1	0	0	–	2	–	0	1	2	0	0	0	–	0	0	6
12	Verstappen	–	0	0	–	–	–	–	2	–	–	0	0	3	–	–	0	–	5
13	Irvine	–	0	0	0	–	3	0	0	–	0	0	0	–	0	0	1		4
14	Zonta	1	0	0	–	0	–	0	–	–	0	0	–	0	0	1	1	0	3
15	De la Rosa	–	0	–	–	–	1	–	–	–	–	1	0	–	–	–	0	–	2
=	Wurz	0	–	0	0	0	0	–	0	0	–	0	0	2	0	–	0		2
NP	Alesi	–	–	0	–	0	–	–	0	–	–	–	–	0	–	0	–		0
NP	Burti	–	–	–	–	–	–	–	–	–	–	0	–	–	–	–	–		0
NP	Diniz	–	0	0	0	–	0	0	0	0	–	0	0	0	0	0	0		0
NP	Gené	0	0	0	0	0	–	0	0	0	–	0	0	0	0	0	0		0
NP	Heidfeld	–	–	0	–	0	DQ	0	–	–	–	0	–	–	–	0	–		0
NP	Herbert	–	–	0	0	0	0	0	0	0	–	–	–	0	0	–	0		0
NP	Mazzacane	–	0	0	0	0	0	–	0	–	0	0	–	0	0	–	0	0	0

CONSTRUCTORS' WORLD CHAMPIONSHIP

		Australia	Brazil	San Marino	Britain	Spain	Europe	Monaco	Canada	France	Austria	Germany	Hungary	Belgium	Italy	United States	Japan	Malaysia	Total
1	Ferrari	16	10	13	4	6	13	6	16	4	4	10	9	6	10	16	13	14	170
2	McLaren	–	–	10	16	16	10	11	3	16	6	10	14	13	6	2	10	9	152
3	Williams	4	3	–	5	3	0	–	0	2	2	3	2	6	4	–	2	–	36
4	Benetton	2	6	0	0	0	2	4	4	0	0	–	0	0	2	0	–	0	20
5	BAR	4	0	2	–	0	–	0	0	3	3	0	0	0	1	4	1	2	20
6	Jordan	–	7	0	1	1	–	0	1	1	–	0	1	1	–	4	0	0	17
7	Arrows	–	0	0	–	–	1	–	2	–	–	1	0	–	–	0	0		7
8	Sauber	–	1	0	0	0	2	0	–	1	2	0	0	0	0	0	0	0	6
9	Jaguar	–	0	0	0	0	3	0	0	0	0	0	0	–	0	0	1		4
NP	Minardi	0	0	0	0	0	–	0	0	0	0	0	0	0	0	0	0	0	0
NP	Prost	0	–	0	0	0	0	–	0	0	–	0	–	0	0	0	0		0

Points: first place: 10 points; second place: 6 points; third place: 4 points; fourth place: 3 points; fifth place: 2 points; sixth place: 1 point. 0 = classified but no world championship points gained   – = retired or did not start   NP = no placing   DQ=disqualified

Statistics

Australian Grand Prix

12 March, Melbourne

Track length 5.269 km (3.274 miles) • **Race distance** 305.602 km (189.892 miles), 58 laps
Lap record 1:30.585 min, Heinz-Harald Frentzen, Williams-Renault, 1997 • **Weather** Sunny and hot • **Spectators** 124,000

RACE RESULTS

	Driver	Team	Pit-stops	Time (hours)	Ave. (mph)
1	M. Schumacher	Ferrari	1	1:34.01.987	121.952
2	Barrichello	Ferrari	2	1:34.13.402	121.706
3	R. Schumacher	Williams-BMW	1	1:34.21.996	121.521
4	Villeneuve	BAR-Honda	1	1:34.46.434	120.999
5	Fisichella	Benetton-Playlife	1	1:34.47.152	120.984
6	Zonta	BAR-Honda	1	1:34.48.455	120.956
7	Wurz	Benetton-Playlife	1	1:34.48.902	120.947
8	Gené	Minardi-Fondmetal	2	1 lap behind	118.359
9	Heidfeld	Prost-Peugeot	1	2 laps behind	117.578
DQ	Salo*	Sauber-Petronas	1	1.34.47.611	120.974

* Disqualified for an infringement of technical regulations after finishing sixth.

RETIREMENTS

Driver	Team	Lap	Reason	Ave. (mph)
Button	Williams-BMW	47	Engine failure	119.771
Diniz	Sauber-Petronas	42	Gearbox failure	115.540
Mazzacane	Minardi-Fondmetal	41	Gearbox failure	115.452
Frentzen	Jordan-Mugen-Honda	40	Gearbox failure	118.896
Trulli	Jordan-Mugen-Honda	36	Broken exhaust	119.657
Alesi	Prost-Peugeot	28	Engine failure	115.600
Hakkinen	McLaren-Mercedes	19	Engine failure	115.500
Verstappen	Arrows-Supertec	17	Withdrawn	100.539
Coulthard	McLaren-Mercedes	12	Engine failure	103.193
De la Rosa	Arrows-Supertec	7	Accident	120.274
Irvine	Jaguar-Ford	7	Accident	120.071
Herbert	Jaguar-Ford	2	Engine failure	89.216

FASTEST LAPS

	Driver	Time (min)		Driver	Time (min)
1	Barrichello	1:31.481	12	Fisichella	1:33.449
2	M. Schumacher	1:31.752	13	Wurz	1:33.459
3	Frentzen	1:32.110	14	Salo	1:33.471
4	Hakkinen	1:32.433	15	Coulthard	1:33.653
5	R. Schumacher	1:32.525	16	Heidfeld	1:34.111
6	Diniz	1:32.977	17	Verstappen	1:34.834
7	Villeneuve	1:33.185	18	Alesi	1:35.088
8	Trulli	1:33.223	19	Mazzacane	1:35.241
9	Gené	1:33.231	20	De la Rosa	1:35.663
10	Button	1:33.351	21	Irvine	1:35.789
11	Zonta	1:33.435	22	Herbert	—

Brazilian Grand Prix

26 March, São Paulo

Track length 4.311 km (2.679 miles) • **Race distance** 306.081 km (190.209 miles), 71 laps
Lap record 1:14.755 min, Michael Schumacher, Ferrari, 2000 • **Weather** Hot and overcast • **Spectators** 105,000

RACE RESULTS

	Driver	Team	Pit-stops	Time (hours)	Ave. (mph)
1	M. Schumacher	Ferrari	2	1:31.35.271	124.551
2	Fisichella	Benetton-Playlife	1	1:32.15.169	123.211
3	Frentzen	Jordan-Mugen-Honda	1	1:32.17.539	123.600
4	Trulli	Jordan-Mugen-Honda	2	1:32.48.051	122.924
5	R. Schumacher	Williams-BMW	1	1 lap behind	122.773
6	Button	Williams-BMW	1	1 lap behind	122.357
7	Verstappen	Arrows-Supertec	1	1 lap behind	121.971
8	De la Rosa	Arrows-Supertec	1	1 lap behind	121.663
9	Zonta	BAR-Honda	1	2 laps behind	121.038
10	Mazzacane	Minardi-Fondmetal	1	2 laps behind	120.466
DQ	Coulthard*	McLaren-Mercedes	1	1:31.39.573	124.454

* Disqualified for an infringement of technical regulations after finishing second.

RETIREMENTS

Driver	Team	Lap	Reason	Ave. (mph)
Herbert	Jaguar-Ford	52	Gearbox failure	121.673
Gené	Minardi-Fondmetal	32	Engine failure	121.123
Hakkinen	McLaren-Mercedes	31	Loss of oil pressure	124.385
Barrichello	Ferrari	28	Hydraulic failure	121.570
Irvine	Jaguar-Ford	21	Accident	121.570
Villeneuve	BAR-Honda	17	Gearbox failure	119.834
Alesi	Prost-Peugeot	12	Engine failure	119.571
Heidfeld	Prost-Peugeot	10	Engine failure	117.527
Wurz	Benetton-Playlife	7	Engine failure	105.004

Diniz and Salo, Sauber-Petronas, withdrew before the race on safety grounds.

FASTEST LAPS

	Driver	Time (min)		Driver	Time (min)
1	M. Schumacher	1:14.755	12	Verstappen	1:16.975
2	Frentzen	1:15.192	13	Gené	1:17.174
3	Hakkinen	1:15.456	14	Mazzacane	1:17.380
4	Barrichello	1:15.632	15	Herbert	1:17.696
5	Coulthard	1:15.633	16	Irvine	1:17.792
6	Fisichella	1:16.002	17	Villeneuve	1:18.379
7	Trulli	1:16.375	18	Alesi	1:18.381
8	Button	1:16.379	19	Heidfeld	1:18.765
9	R. Schumacher	1:16.398	20	Wurz	1:19.821
10	Zonta	1:16.658	21	Diniz	did not start
11	De la Rosa	1:16.967	22	Salo	did not start

San Marino Grand Prix

9 April, Imola

Track length 4.929 km (3.063 miles) • **Race distance** 305.598 km (189.895 miles), 62 laps
Lap record 1:25.531 min, Heinz-Harald Frentzen, Williams-Renault, 1997 • **Weather**
Dry and sunny • **Spectators** 110,000

RACE RESULTS

	Driver	Team	Pit-stops	Time (hours)	Ave. (mph)
1	M. Schumacher	Ferrari	2	1:31:39.776	124.328
2	Hakkinen	McLaren-Mercedes	2	1:31:40.944	124.300
3	Coulthard	McLaren-Mercedes	2	1:32:30.784	123.184
4	Barrichello	Ferrari	2	1:33:09.052	122.341
5	Villeneuve	BAR-Honda	2	1 lap behind	121.898
6	Salo	Sauber-Petronas	2	1 lap behind	121.887
7	Irvine	Jaguar-Ford	2	1 lap behind	121.740
8	Diniz	Sauber-Petronas	2	1 lap behind	121.651
9	Wurz	Benetton-Playlife	1	1 lap behind	121.157
10	Herbert	Jaguar-Ford	1	1 lap behind	121.045
11	Fisichella	Benetton-Playlife	1	1 lap behind	121.032
12	Zonta	BAR-Honda	2	1 lap behind	120.549
13	Mazzacane	Minardi-Fondmetal	2	2 laps behind	118.543
14	Verstappen	Arrows-Supertec	3	3 laps behind	118.193
15	Trulli*	Jordan-Mugen-Honda	2	4 laps behind	121.664

* Retired but assessed because of the distance covered.

RETIREMENTS

Driver	Team	Lap	Reason	Ave. (mph)
De la Rosa	Arrows-Supertec	50	Spun off	120.302
R. Schumacher	Williams-BMW	46	Loss of oil pressure	122.378
Alesi	Prost-Peugeot	36	Hydraulics failure	117.395
Heidfeld	Prost-Peugeot	23	Hydraulics failure	117.721
Button	Williams-BMW	6	Engine failure	115.972
Gené	Minardi-Fondmetal	6	Spun off	115.771
Frentzen	Jordan-Mugen-Honda	5	Gearbox failure	115.095

FASTEST LAPS

	Driver	Time (min)		Driver	Time (min)
1	Hakkinen	1:26.523	12	Verstappen	1:28.842
2	M. Schumacher	1:26.774	13	Fisichella	1:28.884
3	Coulthard	1:27.014	14	Herbert	1:29.049
4	R. Schumacher	1:27.339	15	Wurz	1:29.180
5	Diniz	1:27.814	16	Heidfeld	1:29.350
6	Barrichello	1:27.899	17	De la Rosa	1:29.370
7	Salo	1:28.336	18	Alesi	1:29.719
8	Irvine	1:28.387	19	Mazzacane	1:30.030
9	Trulli	1:28.754	20	Frentzen	1:31.503
10	Zonta	1:28.787	21	Gené	1:31.524
11	Villeneuve	1:28.816	22	Button	1:31.912

British Grand Prix

23 April, Silverstone

Track length 5.142 km (3.194 miles) • **Race distance** 308.52 km (191.64 miles), 60 laps
Lap record 1:24.475 min, Michael Schumacher, Ferrari, 1997 • **Weather** Dry but cloudy
Spectators 100,000

RACE RESULTS

	Driver	Team	Pit-stops	Time (hours)	Ave. (mph)
1	Coulthard	McLaren-Mercedes	1	1:28.50.108	129.438
2	Hakkinen	McLaren-Mercedes	1	1:28.51.585	129.402
3	M. Schumacher	Ferrari	1	1:29.10.025	128.956
4	R. Schumacher	Williams-BMW	2	1:29.31.420	128.443
5	Button	Williams-BMW	2	1:29.47.867	128.050
6	Trulli	Jordan-Mugen-Honda	1	1:30.09.381	127.341
7	Fisichella	Benetton-Playlife	2	1 lap behind	127.204
8	Salo	Sauber-Petronas	2	1 lap behind	126.687
9	Wurz	Benetton-Playlife	2	1 lap behind	126.643
10	Alesi	Prost-Peugeot	2	1 lap behind	126.589
11	Diniz	Sauber-Petronas	2	1 lap behind	126.572
12	Herbert	Jaguar-Ford	2	1 lap behind	126.541
13	Irvine	Jaguar-Ford	2	1 lap behind	126.471
14	Gené	Minardi-Fondmetal	2	1 lap behind	126.229
15	Mazzacane	Minardi-Fondmetal	2	1 lap behind	126.079
16	Villeneuve*	BAR-Honda	1	4 laps behind	127.249
17	Frentzen*	Jordan-Mugen-Honda	2	6 laps behind	127.063

* Retired but assessed because of the distance covered.

RETIREMENTS

Driver	Team	Lap	Reason	Ave. (mph)
Heidfeld	Prost-Peugeot	52	Loss of oil pressure	125.985
Zonta	BAR-Honda	37	Spun off	126.145
Barrichello	Ferrari	36	Hydraulic failure	128.548
De la Rosa	Arrows-Supertec	27	Electrical failure	124.554
Verstappen	Arrows-Supertec	21	Electrical failure	121.186

FASTEST LAPS

	Driver	Time (min)		Driver	Time (min)
1	Hakkinen	1:26.217	12	Diniz	1:28.037
2	M. Schumacher	1:26.428	13	Villeneuve	1:28.093
3	R. Schumacher	1:26.998	14	Fisichella	1:28.116
4	Coulthard	1:27.093	15	Salo	1:28.178
5	Frentzen	1:27.286	16	Alesi	1:28.388
6	Barrichello	1:27.496	17	Wurz	1:28.487
7	Button	1:27.631	18	Gené	1:28.557
8	Zonta	1:27.655	19	Mazzacane	1:28.665
9	Trulli	1:27.824	20	Heidfeld	1:28.803
10	Herbert	1:28.001	21	De la Rosa	1:28.867
11	Irvine	1:28.009	22	Verstappen	1:29.546

Spanish Grand Prix
7 May, Barcelona

Track length 4.727 km (2.937 miles) • **Race distance** 307.255 km (190.905 miles), 65 laps
Lap record 1:22.242 min, Giancarlo Fisichella, Jordan-Peugeot, 1997 • **Weather** Dry but overcast • **Spectators** 100,000

RACE RESULTS

	Driver	Team	Pit-stops	Time (hours)	Ave. (mph)
1	Hakkinen	McLaren-Mercedes	2	1:33.55.390	122.016
2	Coulthard	McLaren-Mercedes	2	1:34.11.456	121.669
3	Barrichello	Ferrari	2	1:34.24.502	121.389
4	R. Schumacher	Williams-BMW	2	1:34.32.701	121.213
5	M. Schumacher	Ferrari	3	1:34.43.373	120.986
6	Frentzen	Jordan-Mugen-Honda	2	1:35.17.315	120.267
7	Salo	Sauber-Petronas	2	1 lap behind	120.122
8	Zonta	BAR-Honda	2	1 lap behind	120.108
9	Fisichella	Benetton-Playlife	2	1 lap behind	119.881
10	Wurz	Benetton-Playlife	2	1 lap behind	119.457
11	Irvine	Jaguar-Ford	2	1 lap behind	119.436
12	Trulli	Jordan-Mugen-Honda	2	1 lap behind	119.213
13	Herbert	Jaguar-Ford	3	1 lap behind	118.795
14	Gené	Minardi-Fondmetal	4	2 laps behind	118.077
15	Mazzacane	Minardi-Fondmetal	3	2 laps behind	117.376
16	Heidfeld	Prost-Peugeot	4	3 laps behind	115.976
17	Button*	Williams-BMW	2	4 laps behind	120.509

*Retired but assessed because of the distance covered.

RETIREMENTS

Driver	Team	Lap	Reason	Ave. (mph)
Verstappen	Arrows-Supertec	26	Gearbox failure	119.972
Villeneuve	BAR-Honda	22	Engine failure	120.614
Alesi	Prost-Peugeot	2	Accident	104.313
De la Rosa	Arrows-Supertec	2	Accident	104.019
Diniz	Sauber-Petronas	1	Spun off	—

FASTEST LAPS

	Driver	Time (min)		Driver	Time (min)
1	Hakkinen	1:24.470	12	Irvine	1:26.239
2	M. Schumacher	1:24.517	13	Zonta	1:26.241
3	Coulthard	1:24.684	14	Fisichella	1:26.352
4	Button	1:24.729	15	Heidfeld	1:26.663
5	Frentzen	1:25.183	16	Herbert	1:26.685
6	Barrichello	1:25.288	17	Villeneuve	1:26.701
7	R. Schumacher	1:25.326	18	Verstappen	1:27.152
8	Trulli	1:25.806	19	Mazzacane	1:27.538
9	Salo	1:25.896	20	Alesi	—
10	Gené	1:25.915	21	De la Rosa	—
11	Wurz	1:26.147	22	Diniz	—

European Grand Prix
21 May, Nürburgring

Track length 4.556 km (2.831 miles) • **Race distance** 305.252 km (189.677 miles), 67 laps
Lap record 1:18.805 min, Heinz-Harald Frentzen, Williams-Renault, 1997 • **Weather** Dry at first, then wet • **Spectators** 142,000

RACE RESULTS

	Driver	Team	Pit-stops	Time (hours)	Ave. (mph)
1	M. Schumacher	Ferrari	2	1:42.00.307	111.585
2	Hakkinen	McLaren-Mercedes	2	1:42.14.129	111.334
3	Coulthard	McLaren-Mercedes	2	1 lap behind	109.786
4	Barrichello	Ferrari	3	1 lap behind	109.758
5	Fisichella	Benetton-Playlife	2	1 lap behind	109.539
6	De la Rosa	Arrows-Supertec	2	1 lap behind	108.637
7	Diniz	Sauber-Petronas	2	2 laps behind	107.702
8	Mazzacane	Minardi-Fondmetal	2	2 laps behind	107.473
9	Alesi	Prost-Peugeot	4	2 laps behind	106.865
10	Button*	Williams-BMW	2	5 laps behind	107.978
11	Herbert*	Jaguar-Ford	2	6 laps behind	108.091
12	Wurz*	Benetton-Playlife	2	6 laps behind	108.033

* Retired but still assessed because of the distance travelled.

RETIREMENTS

Driver	Team	Lap	Reason	Ave. (mph)
Zonta	BAR-Honda	52	Spun off	107.138
Gené	Minardi-Fondmetal	48	Broken accelerator	107.014
Villeneuve	BAR-Honda	47	Engine failure	109.141
Irvine	Jaguar-Ford	30	Accident	109.789
Verstappen	Arrows-Supertec	30	Accident	109.784
R. Schumacher	Williams-BMW	30	Accident	109.767
Salo	Sauber-Petronas	28	Broken driveshaft	109.434
Frentzen	Jordan-Mugen-Honda	3	Engine failure	100.788
Trulli	Jordan-Mugen-Honda	1	Accident	—

Heidfeld, Prost-Peugeot, was disqualified for being underweight in qualifying.

FASTEST LAPS

	Driver	Time (min)		Driver	Time (min)
1	M. Schumacher	1:22.269	12	Alesi	1:23.898
2	Hakkinen	1:22.288	13	Irvine	1:24.008
3	Coulthard	1:22.289	14	Gené	1:24.018
4	Barrichello	1:22.339	15	Salo	1:24.346
5	De la Rosa	1:23.125	16	Zonta	1:24.620
6	Fisichella	1:23.255	17	Herbert	1:24.715
7	Verstappen	1:23.369	18	Mazzacane	1:24.772
8	Villeneuve	1:23.390	19	Diniz	1:24.798
9	Wurz	1:23.485	20	Frentzen	1:24.937
10	Button	1:23.688	21	Trulli	—
11	R. Schumacher	1:23.802	22	Heidfeld	—

Monaco Grand Prix

4 June, Monte Carlo

Track length 3.366 km (2.092 miles) • **Race distance** 262.548 km (163.176 miles), 78 laps
Lap record 1:22.259 min, Mika Hakkinen, McLaren-Mercedes, 1999 • **Weather** Dry and sunny • **Spectators** 120,000

R A C E   R E S U L T S

	Driver	Team	Pit-stops	Time (hours)	Ave. (mph)
1	Coulthard	McLaren-Mercedes	1	1:49.28.213	89.541
2	Barrichello	Ferrari	1	1:49.44.102	89.325
3	Fisichella	Benetton-Playlife	1	1:49.46.735	89.289
4	Irvine	Jaguar-Ford	1	1:50.34.137	88.651
5	Salo	Sauber-Petronas	1	1:50.48.988	88.453
6	Hakkinen	McLaren-Mercedes	1	1 lap behind	88.331
7	Villeneuve	BAR-Honda	1	1 lap behind	87.860
8	Heidfeld	Prost-Peugeot	1	1 lap behind	87.441
9	Herbert	Jaguar-Ford	2	2 laps behind	86.261
10	Frentzen*	Jordan-Mugen-Honda	1	8 laps behind	89.303

* Retired but still assessed because of the distance travelled.

R E T I R E M E N T S

Driver	Team	Lap	Reason	Ave. (mph)
Verstappen	Arrows-Supertec	61	Accident	87.033
M. Schumacher	Ferrari	56	Suspension failure	89.681
Zonta	BAR-Honda	49	Accident	86.948
R. Schumacher	Williams-BMW	38	Accident	88.708
Trulli	Jordan-Mugen-Honda	37	Gearbox failure	88.832
Diniz	Sauber-Petronas	31	Accident	87.019
Alesi	Prost-Peugeot	30	Transmission failure	88.386
Mazzacane	Minardi-Fondmetal	23	Accident	86.383
Gené	Minardi-Fondmetal	22	Gearbox failure	86.226
Wurz	Benetton-Playlife	19	Accident	86.074
Button	Williams-BMW	17	Engine failure	85.639
De la Rosa	Arrows-Supertec	—	Accident	—

F A S T E S T   L A P S

	Driver	Time (min)		Driver	Time (min)
1	Hakkinen	1:21.571	12	Trulli	1:23.466
2	Coulthard	1:21.787	13	Zonta	1:23.514
3	Fisichella	1:21.905	14	R. Schumacher	1:23.769
4	Barrichello	1:21.910	15	Alesi	1:23.949
5	M. Schumacher	1:21.912	16	Gené	1:24.351
6	Frentzen	1:22.123	17	Verstappen	1:24.486
7	Irvine	1:22.424	18	Diniz	1:24.590
8	Salo	1:22.634	19	Mazzacane	1:25.039
9	Herbert	1:23.245	20	Wurz	1:25.484
10	Heidfeld	1:23.261	21	Button	1:25.740
11	Villeneuve	1:23.393	22	De la Rosa	—

Canadian Grand Prix

18 June, Montreal

Track length 4.421 km (2.747 miles) • **Race distance** 305.049 km (189.543 miles), 69 laps
Lap record 1:19.379 min, Michael Schumacher, Ferrari, 1998 • **Weather** Dry at first, then wet • **Spectators** 110,000

R A C E   R E S U L T S

	Driver	Team	Pit-stops	Time (hours)	Ave. (mph)
1	M. Schumacher	Ferrari	2	1:41.12.313	112.398
2	Barrichello	Ferrari	2	1:41.12.487	112.395
3	Fisichella	Benetton-Playlife	1	1:41.27.678	112.115
4	Hakkinen	McLaren-Mercedes	2	1:41.30.874	112.056
5	Verstappen	Arrows-Supertec	2	1:42.04.521	111.439
6	Trulli	Jordan-Mugen-Honda	2	1:42.14.000	111.268
7	Coulthard	McLaren-Mercedes	3	1:42.14.529	111.261
8	Zonta	BAR-Honda	2	1:42.22.768	111.109
9	Wurz	Benetton-Playlife	2	1:42.32.212	110.939
10	Diniz	Sauber-Petronas	2	1:43.31.857	110.318
11	Button	Williams-BMW	2	1 lap behind	110.747
12	Mazzacane	Minardi-Fondmetal	2	1 lap behind	109.114
13	Irvine	Jaguar-Ford	2	3 laps behind	105.817
14	R. Schumacher*	Williams-BMW	3	5 laps behind	112.224
15	Villeneuve*	BAR-Honda	2	5 laps behind	112.189
16	Gené*	Minardi-Fondmetal	2	5 laps behind	111.347

* Retired but still assessed because of the distance travelled.

R E T I R E M E N T S

Driver	Team	Lap	Reason	Ave. (mph)
De la Rosa	Arrows-Supertec	48	Accident	115.689
Salo	Sauber-Petronas	42	Engine failure	119.032
Alesi	Prost-Peugeot	38	Hydraulic failure	118.352
Heidfeld	Prost-Peugeot	34	Engine failure	118.154
Frentzen	Jordan-Mugen-Honda	32	Brake failure	119.858
Herbert	Jaguar-Ford	14	Gearbox failure	117.789

F A S T E S T   L A P S

	Driver	Time (min)		Driver	Time (min)
1	Hakkinen	1:19.049	12	Zonta	1:20.686
2	Barrichello	1:19.235	13	Verstappen	1:20.693
3	M. Schumacher	1:19.812	14	Irvine	1:20.693
4	Coulthard	1:19.947	15	Salo	1:20.696
5	Fisichella	1:20.399	16	Button	1:20.781
6	Trulli	1:20.479	17	De la Rosa	1:20.842
7	Diniz	1:20.494	18	Alesi	1:20.889
8	R. Schumacher	1:20.520	19	Heidfeld	1:21.096
9	Villeneuve	1:20.533	20	Frentzen	1:21.110
10	Gené	1:20.547	21	Mazzacane	1:21.196
11	Wurz	1:20.625	22	Herbert	1:22.369

French Grand Prix

2 July, Magny-Cours

Track length 4.250 km (2.641 miles) • **Race distance** 306.029 km (190.152 miles), 72 laps
Lap record 1:17.070 min, Nigel Mansell, Williams-Renault, 1992 • **Weather** Hot and humid • **Spectators** 110,000

RACE RESULTS

	Driver	Team	Pit-stops	Time (hours)	Ave. (mph)
1	Coulthard	McLaren-Mercedes	2	1:38.06.538	116.283
2	Hakkinen	McLaren-Mercedes	2	1:38.20.286	115.993
3	Barrichello	Ferrari	2	1:38.37.947	115.647
4	Villeneuve	BAR-Honda	2	1:39.06.860	115.084
5	R. Schumacher	Williams-BMW	3	1:39.09.519	115.034
6	Trulli	Jordan-Mugen-Honda	2	1:39.21.143	114.808
7	Frentzen	Jordan-Mugen-Honda	2	1 lap behind	114.346
8	Button	Williams-BMW	2	1 lap behind	114.331
9	Fisichella	Benetton-Playlife	2	1 lap behind	114.299
10	Salo	Sauber-Petronas	2	1 lap behind	113.511
11	Diniz	Sauber-Petronas	2	1 lap behind	113.231
12	Heidfeld	Prost-Peugeot	3	1 lap behind	113.208
13	Irvine	Jaguar-Ford	4	2 laps behind	113.043
14	Alesi	Prost-Peugeot	2	2 laps behind	112.028
15	Gené	Minardi-Fondmetal	2	2 laps behind	112.019

RETIREMENTS

Driver	Team	Lap	Reason	Ave. (mph)
M. Schumacher	Ferrari	59	Engine failure	116.128
De la Rosa	Arrows-Supertec	46	Transmission failure	111.662
Wurz	Benetton-Playlife	35	Spun off	112.705
Mazzacane	Minardi-Fondmetal	32	Spun off	112.031
Verstappen	Arrows-Supertec	26	Gearbox failure	112.868
Herbert	Jaguar-Ford	21	Clutch failure	110.065
Zonta	BAR-Honda	17	Brake failure	101.077

FASTEST LAPS

	Driver	Time (min)		Driver	Time (min)
1	Coulthard	1:19.479	12	Frentzen	1:21.255
2	M. Schumacher	1:19.656	13	De la Rosa	1:21.506
3	Irvine	1:19.708	14	Salo	1:21.725
4	Hakkinen	1:19.746	15	Diniz	1:21.753
5	Barrichello	1:20.225	16	Herbert	1:21.901
6	Villeneuve	1:20.857	17	Alesi	1:22.293
7	R. Schumacher	1:20.908	18	Gené	1:22.420
8	Fisichella	1:20.958	19	Wurz	1:22.481
9	Trulli	1:21.071	20	Verstappen	1:22.498
10	Heidfeld	1:21.115	21	Zonta	1:22.563
11	Button	1:21.151	22	Mazzacane	1:22.639

Austrian Grand Prix

16 July, A1-Ring

Track length 4.319 km (2.684 miles) • **Race distance** 306.640 km (190.543 miles), 71 laps
Lap record 1:11.814 min, Jacques Villeneuve, Williams-Renault, 1997 • **Weather** Warm and sunny • **Spectators** 120,000

RACE RESULTS

	Driver	Team	Pit-stops	Time (hours)	Ave. (mph)
1	Hakkinen	McLaren-Mercedes	1	1:28.15.818	129.765
2	Coulthard	McLaren-Mercedes	1	1.28.28.353	129.459
3	Barrichello	Ferrari	1	1:28.46.613	129.015
4	Villeneuve	BAR-Honda	1	1 lap behind	127.392
5	Button	Williams-BMW	1	1 lap behind	127.308
6	Salo	Sauber-Petronas	1	1 lap behind	127.285
7	Herbert	Jaguar-Ford	1	1 lap behind	127.274
8	Gené	Minardi-Fondmetal	1	1 lap behind	127.065
9	Diniz	Sauber-Petronas	1	1 lap behind	127.050
10	Wurz	Benetton-Playlife	3	1 lap behind	127.032
11	Burti	Jaguar-Ford	1	2 laps behind	125.736
12	Mazzacane	Minardi-Fondmetal	1	3 laps behind	124.281

RETIREMENTS

Driver	Team	Lap	Reason	Ave. (mph)
Zonta	BAR-Honda	59	Engine failure	125.962
R. Schumacher	Williams-BMW	53	Brake failure	108.765
Heidfeld	Prost-Peugeot	42	Accident	125.086
Alesi	Prost-Peugeot	42	Accident	125.076
De la Rosa	Arrows-Supertec	33	Gearbox failure	126.686
Verstappen	Arrows-Supertec	15	Engine failure	117.795
Frentzen	Jordan-Mugen-Honda	5	Engine failure	106.064
Trulli	Jordan-Mugen-Honda	1	Accident	—
Fisichella	Benetton-Playlife	1	Accident	—
M. Schumacher	Ferrari	1	Accident	—

FASTEST LAPS

	Driver	Time (min)		Driver	Time (min)
1	Coulthard	1:11.783	12	Herbert	1:13.613
2	Hakkinen	1:11.837	13	Gené	1:13.626
3	Barrichello	1:11.887	14	Salo	1:13.674
4	Villeneuve	1:12.630	15	Mazzacane	1:13.733
5	R. Schumacher	1:12.811	16	Alesi	1:14.039
6	Zonta	1:12.855	17	Burti	1:14.098
7	Diniz	1:12.955	18	Verstappen	1:14.227
8	Button	1:12.964	19	Frentzen	1:16.588
9	Wurz	1:13.317	20	Trulli	—
10	De la Rosa	1:13.490	21	Fisichella	—
11	Heidfeld	1:13.593	22	M. Schumacher	—

Marlboro
tic tac

German Grand Prix

30 July, Hockenheim

Track length 6.822 km (4.239 miles) • **Race distance** 307.305 km (190.755 miles), 45 laps
Lap record 1:45.270 min, David Coulthard, McLaren-Mercedes, 1999 • **Weather** Mixed
wet and dry • **Spectators** 120,000

RACE RESULTS

	Driver	Team	Pit-stops	Time (hours)	Ave. (mph)
1	Barrichello	Ferrari	2	1:25.34.418	133.835
2	Hakkinen	McLaren-Mercedes	2	1:25.41.870	133.641
3	Coulthard	McLaren-Mercedes	2	1:25.55.586	133.285
4	Button	Williams-BMW	2	1:25.57.103	133.246
5	Salo	Sauber-Petronas	2	1:26.01.530	133.132
6	De la Rosa	Arrows-Supertec	2	1:26.03.497	133.081
7	R. Schumacher	Williams-BMW	2	1:26.05.316	133.034
8	Villeneuve	BAR-Honda	2	1:26.21.955	132.607
9	Trulli	Jordan-Mugen-Honda	2	1:26.25.319	132.521
10	Irvine	Jaguar-Ford	2	1:26.54.082	131.790
10	Mazzacane	Minardi-Fondmetal	2	1:27.03.922	131.542
10	Heidfeld*	Prost-Peugeot	2	5 laps behind	132.952

* Retired but still assessed because of the distance travelled.

RETIREMENTS

Driver	Team	Lap	Reason	Ave. (mph)
Frentzen	Jordan-Mugen-Honda	40	Electrical failure	134.167
Verstappen	Arrows-Supertec	40	Spun off	133.688
Zonta	BAR-Honda	38	Spun off	134.921
Gené	Minardi-Fondmetal	34	Engine failure	135.369
Wurz	Benetton-Playlife	32	Spun off	134.991
Diniz	Sauber-Petronas	30	Accident	137.015
Alesi	Prost-Peugeot	30	Accident	136.981
Herbert	Jaguar-Ford	13	Gearbox failure	140.270
M. Schumacher	Ferrari	1	Accident	—
Fisichella	Benetton-Playlife	1	Accident	—

FASTEST LAPS

	Driver	Time (min)		Driver	Time (min)
1	Barrichello	1:44.300	12	Salo	1:47.129
2	Coulthard	1:44.579	13	Heidfeld	1:47.140
3	Frentzen	1:44.614	14	Verstappen	1:47.156
4	Hakkinen	1:44.698	15	Gené	1:48.158
5	Trulli	1:45.754	16	Zonta	1:47.248
6	De la Rosa	1:46.234	17	Wurz	1:47.269
7	Villeneuve	1:46.374	18	Herbert	1:47.332
8	Diniz	1:46.639	19	Mazzacane	1:47.448
9	R. Schumacher	1:46.685	20	Irvine	1:47.570
10	Alesi	1:47.001	21	M. Schumacher	—
11	Button	1:47.073	22	Fisichella	—

Hungarian Grand Prix

13 August, Hungaroring

Track length 3.968 km (2.465 miles) • **Race distance** 305.536 km (189.805 miles),
77 laps • **Lap record** 1:18.308 min, Nigel Mansell, Williams-Renault, 1992 • **Weather**
Dry and hot • **Spectators** 120,000

RACE RESULTS

	Driver	Team	Pit-stops	Time (hours)	Ave. (mph)
1	Hakkinen	McLaren-Mercedes	2	1:45.33.869	108.100
2	M. Schumacher	Ferrari	2	1:45.41.785	107.970
3	Coulthard	McLaren-Mercedes	2	1:45.42.324	107.960
4	Barrichello	Ferrari	2	1:46.18.026	107.350
5	R. Schumacher	Williams-BMW	2	1:46.24.306	107.250
6	Frentzen	Jordan-Mugen-Honda	2	1:46.41.968	106.950
7	Trulli	Jordan-Mugen-Honda	1	1 lap behind	106.250
8	Irvine	Jaguar-Ford	2	1 lap behind	106.240
9	Button	Williams-BMW	2	1 lap behind	106.170
10	Salo	Sauber-Petronas	2	1 lap behind	105.600
11	Wurz	Benetton-Playlife	2	1 lap behind	105.480
12	Villeneuve	BAR-Honda	2	2 laps behind	105.250
13	Verstappen	Arrows-Supertec	2	2 laps behind	104.630
14	Zonta	BAR-Honda	2	2 laps behind	103.930
15	Gené	Minardi-Fondmetal	2	3 laps behind	103.400
16	De la Rosa	Arrows-Supertec	1	4 laps behind	102.380

RETIREMENTS

Driver	Team	Lap	Reason	Ave. (mph)
Mazzacane	Minardi-Fondmetal	69	Engine failure	102.510
Herbert	Jaguar-Ford	68	Gearbox failure	103.810
Diniz	Sauber-Petronas	63	Engine failure	105.950
Fisichella	Benetton-Playlife	32	Brake failure	95.090
Heidfeld	Prost-Peugeot	23	Electrical failure	104.070
Alesi	Prost-Peugeot	12	Suspension failure	78.530

FASTEST LAPS

	Driver	Time (min)		Driver	Time (min)
1	Hakkinen	1:20.028	12	Diniz	1:21.491
2	Barrichello	1:20.520	13	Irvine	1:21.572
3	Frentzen	1:20.640	14	Verstappen	1:22.266
4	Coulthard	1:20.641	15	Herbert	1:22.439
5	M. Schumacher	1:20.762	16	Zonta	1:22.633
6	Villeneuve	1:21.163	17	Fisichella	1:22.933
7	R. Schumacher	1:21.211	18	Gené	1:23.388
8	Salo	1:21.372	19	Heidfeld	1:23.744
9	Button	1:21.423	20	De la Rosa	1:23.820
10	Wurz	1:21.483	21	Mazzacane	1:23.912
11	Trulli	1:21.483	22	Alesi	1:24.106

Belgian Grand Prix
27 August, Spa-Francorchamps

Track length 6.968 km (4.330 miles) • **Race distance** 306.597 km (190.516 miles), 44 laps
Lap record 1:51.095 min, Alain Prost, Williams-Renault, 1993 • **Weather** Overcast
Spectators 100,000

RACE RESULTS

	Driver	Team	Pit-stops	Time (hours)	Ave. (mph)
1	Hakkinen	McLaren-Mercedes	2	1:28.14.494	129.541
2	M. Schumacher	Ferrari	2	1:28.15.597	129.515
3	R. Schumacher	Williams-BMW	2	1:28.52.590	128.616
4	Coulthard	McLaren-Mercedes	2	1:28.57.774	128.409
5	Button	Williams-BMW	2	1:29.04.408	128.332
6	Frentzen	Jordan-Mugen-Honda	2	1:29.10.478	128.186
7	Villeneuve	BAR-Honda	2	1:29.26.874	127.795
8	Herbert	Jaguar-Ford	2	1:29.42.302	127.428
9	Salo	Sauber-Petronas	2	1:29.43.164	127.408
10	Irvine	Jaguar-Ford	2	1:29.46.049	127.340
11	Diniz	Sauber-Petronas	2	1:29.48.617	127.280
12	Zonta	BAR-Honda	2	1 lap behind	126.323
13	Wurz	Benetton-Playlife	2	1 lap behind	125.541
14	Gené	Minardi-Fondmetal	3	1 lap behind	125.186
15	Verstappen	Arrows-Supertec	3	1 lap behind	124.328
16	De la Rosa	Arrows-Supertec	4	2 laps behind	123.565
17	Mazzacane	Minardi-Fondmetal	2	2 laps behind	121.873

RETIREMENTS

Driver	Team	Lap	Reason	Ave. (mph)
Barrichello	Ferrari	33	Out of fuel	126.648
Alesi	Prost-Peugeot	33	Fuel leak	125.617
Heidfeld	Prost-Peugeot	13	Gearbox failure	114.643
Fisichella	Benetton-Playlife	9	Electrical failure	108.790
Trulli	Jordan-Mugen-Honda	5	Accident	104.690

FASTEST LAPS

	Driver	Time (min)		Driver	Time (min)
1	Barrichello	1:53.803	12	Irvine	1:55.603
2	Coulthard	1:54.131	13	Alesi	1:55.954
3	M. Schumacher	1:54.252	14	Wurz	1:56.726
4	Hakkinen	1:54.469	15	De la Rosa	1:56.770
5	Frentzen	1:54.966	16	Gené	1:57.261
6	Salo	1:55.110	17	Mazzacane	1:57.263
7	Diniz	1:55.153	18	Zonta	1:57.269
8	Button	1:55.425	19	Verstappen	1:57.432
9	R. Schumacher	1:55.473	20	Heidfeld	1:58.831
10	Villeneuve	1:55.511	21	Fisichella	2:02.148
11	Herbert	1:55.603	22	Trulli	2:07.154

Italian Grand Prix
10 September, Monza

Track length 5.769 km (3.585 miles) • **Race distance** 305.757 km (190.005 miles), 53 laps
Lap record 1:24.808 min, Mika Hakkinen, McLaren-Mercedes, 1997 • **Weather** Dry and sunny • **Spectators** 110,000

RACE RESULTS

	Driver	Team	Pit-stops	Time (hours)	Ave. (mph)
1	M. Schumacher	Ferrari	1	1:27.31.638	130.672
2	Hakkinen	McLaren-Mercedes	1	1:27.35.448	130.578
3	R. Schumacher	Williams-BMW	1	1:28.24.070	129.380
4	Verstappen	Arrows-Supertec	1	1:28.31.576	129.197
5	Wurz	Benetton-Playlife	1	1:28.39.064	129.016
6	Zonta	BAR-Honda	3	1:28.40.930	128.970
7	Salo	Sauber-Petronas	3	1 lap behind	128.086
8	Diniz	Sauber-Petronas	2	1 lap behind	127.943
9	Gené	Minardi-Fondmetal	1	1 lap behind	127.787
10	Mazzacane	Minardi-Fondmetal	1	1 lap behind	127.380
11	Fisichella	Benetton-Playlife	1	1 lap behind	126.751
12	Alesi	Prost-Peugeot	1	2 laps behind	125.234

RETIREMENTS

Driver	Team	Lap	Reason	Ave. (mph)
Heidfeld	Prost-Peugeot	16	Spun off	99.131
Villeneuve	BAR-Honda	15	Electrical failure	97.429
Button	Williams-BMW	11	Accident	89.236
Herbert	Jaguar-Ford	2	Accident	47.927
Barrichello	Ferrari	1	Accident	—
Coulthard	McLaren-Mercedes	1	Accident	—
Frentzen	Jordan-Mugen-Honda	1	Accident	—
Trulli	Jordan-Mugen-Honda	1	Accident	—
De la Rosa	Arrows-Supertec	1	Accident	—
Irvine	Jaguar-Ford	1	Accident	—

FASTEST LAPS

	Driver	Time (min)		Driver	Time (min)
1	Hakkinen	1:25.595	12	Gené	1:28.131
2	M. Schumacher	1:25.663	13	Mazzacane	1:28.299
3	Zonta	1:26.433	14	Heidfeld	1:29.580
4	R. Schumacher	1:26.636	15	Button	2:27.131
5	Fisichella	1:26.731	16	Herbert	—
6	Wurz	1:26.869	17	Barrichello	—
7	Verstappen	1:27.033	18	Coulthard	—
8	Diniz	1:27.215	19	Trulli	—
9	Salo	1:27.297	20	Frentzen	—
10	Alesi	1:27.978	21	De la Rosa	—
11	Villeneuve	1:28.038	22	Irvine	—

United States Grand Prix
24 September, Indianapolis

Track length 4.194 km (2.605 miles) • **Race distance** 306.2 km (190.165 miles), 73 laps
Lap record 1:14.711 min, David Coulthard, McLaren-Mercedes, 2000 • **Weather** Dry and cloudy • **Spectators** 220,000

RACE RESULTS

	Driver	Team	Pit-stops	Time (hours)	Ave. (mph)
1	M. Schumacher	Ferrari	2	1:36.30.883	118.893
2	Barrichello	Ferrari	2	1:36.43.001	118.645
3	Frentzen	Jordan-Mugen-Honda	2	1:36.48.251	118.537
4	Villeneuve	BAR-Honda	2	1:36.48.819	118.526
5	Coulthard	McLaren-Mercedes	3	1:36.59.695	118.304
6	Zonta	BAR-Honda	2	1:37.22.577	117.841
7	Irvine	Jaguar-Ford	2	1:37.41.998	117.450
8	Diniz	Sauber-Petronas	3	1 lap behind	117.251
9	Heidfeld	Prost-Peugeot	2	1 lap behind	117.134
10	Wurz	Benetton-Playlife	2	1 lap behind	117.105
11	Herbert	Jaguar-Ford	2	1 lap behind	117.081
12	Gené	Minardi-Fondmetal	2	1 lap behind	116.584

RETIREMENTS

Driver	Team	Lap	Reason	Ave. (mph)
Alesi	Prost-Peugeot	65	Engine failure	116.491
Mazzacane	Minardi-Fondmetal	60	Engine failure	115.010
R. Schumacher	Williams-BMW	59	Pneumatic failure	115.062
De la Rosa	Arrows-Supertec	46	Gearbox failure	114.221
Fisichella	Benetton-Supertec	45	Gearbox failure	112.923
Verstappen	Arrows-Supertec	35	Accident	114.191
Hakkinen	McLaren-Mercedes	26	Engine failure	112.792
Salo	Sauber-Petronas	19	Spun off	106.801
Button	Williams-BMW	15	Engine failure	106.174
Trulli	Jordan-Mugen-Honda	13	Suspension failure	99.235

FASTEST LAPS

	Driver	Time (min)		Driver	Time (min)
1	Coulthard	1:14.711	12	Herbert	1:15.812
2	Barrichello	1:14.822	13	Gené	1:16.044
3	M. Schumacher	1:14.901	14	Heidfeld	1:16.074
4	Villeneuve	1:15.117	15	Alesi	1:16.124
5	Diniz	1:15.305	16	Fisichella	1:16.234
6	Frentzen	1:15.521	17	Verstappen	1:16.252
7	Wurz	1:15.560	18	De la Rosa	1:16.276
8	R. Schumacher	1:15.598	19	Mazzacane	1:16.711
9	Irvine	1:15.675	20	Salo	1:20.244
10	Hakkinen	1:15.773	21	Button	1:22.977
11	Zonta	1:15.812	22	Trulli	1:24.770

Japanese Grand Prix
8 October, Suzuka

Track length 5.864 km (3.642 miles) • **Race distance** 310.772 km (193.026 miles), 53 laps
Lap record 1:38.942 min, Heinz-Harald Frentzen, Williams-Renault, 1997 • **Weather** Dry at first, then wet • **Spectators** 110,000

RACE RESULTS

	Driver	Team	Pit-stops	Time (hours)	Ave. (mph)
1	M. Schumacher	Ferrari	2	1:29.53.435	128.830
2	Hakkinen	McLaren-Mercedes	2	1:29.55.272	128.780
3	Coulthard	McLaren-Mercedes	2	1:31.03.349	127.180
4	Barrichello	Ferrari	2	1:31.12.625	126.960
5	Button	Williams-BMW	2	1:31.19.129	126.810
6	Villeneuve	BAR-Honda	2	1 lap behind	126.200
7	Herbert	Jaguar-Ford	2	1 lap behind	126.180
8	Irvine	Jaguar-Ford	2	1 lap behind	126.140
9	Zonta	BAR-Honda	2	1 lap behind	125.170
10	Salo	Sauber-Petronas	2	1 lap behind	124.650
11	Diniz	Sauber-Petronas	2	1 lap behind	124.490
12	De la Rosa	Arrows-Supertec	2	1 lap behind	124.470
13	Trulli	Jordan-Mugen-Honda	2	1 lap behind	124.390
14	Fisichella	Benetton-Playlife	1	1 lap behind	124.380
15	Mazzacane	Minardi-Fondmetal	2	2 laps behind	121.740

RETIREMENTS

Driver	Team	Lap	Reason	Ave. (mph)
Gené	Minardi-Fondmetal	47	Accident	123.740
Heidfeld	Prost-Peugeot	42	Engine failure	126.770
R. Schumacher	Williams-BMW	42	Hydraulic failure	121.030
Wurz	Benetton-Playlife	38	Engine failure	123.390
Frentzen	Jordan-Mugen-Honda	30	Brake failure	126.690
Alesi	Prost-Peugeot	20	Gearbox failure	126.120
Verstappen	Arrows-Supertec	10	Gearbox failure	122.030

FASTEST LAPS

	Driver	Time (min)		Driver	Time (min)
1	Hakkinen	1:39.189	12	Frentzen	1:41.185
2	M. Schumacher	1:39.443	13	Herbert	1:41.226
3	Coulthard	1:40.058	14	Salo	1:41.634
4	Barrichello	1:40.218	15	De la Rosa	1:42.079
5	Button	1:40.699	16	Heidfeld	1:42.356
6	Villeneuve	1:40.739	17	Fisichella	1:42.416
7	R. Schumacher	1:40.900	18	Alesi	1:42.737
8	Trulli	1:40.967	19	Verstappen	1:42.786
9	Zonta	1:40.980	20	Wurz	1:42.795
10	Diniz	1:41.002	21	Gené	1:42.815
11	Irvine	1:41.154	22	Mazzacane	1:43.997

Malaysian Grand Prix

22 October, Sepang

Track length 5.542 km (3.444 miles) • **Race distance** 310.378 km (192.865 miles), 56 laps
Lap record 1:38.543 min, Mika Hakkinen, McLaren-Mercedes, 2000 • **Weather** Hot and humid **Spectators** 100,000

R A C E   R E S U L T S

	Driver	Team	Pit-stops	Time (hours)	Ave. (mph)
1	M. Schumacher	Ferrari	2	1:35.54.235	121.374
2	Coulthard	McLaren-Mercedes	2	1:35.54.967	121.358
3	Barrichello	Ferrari	2	1:36.13.176	120.986
4	Hakkinen	McLaren-Mercedes	2	1:36.30.004	120.635
5	Villeneuve	BAR	2	1:37.05.427	119.901
6	Irvine	Jaguar-Ford	2	1:37.06.803	119.862
7	Wurz	Benetton-Playlife	2	1:37.33.549	119.519
8	Salo	Sauber-Petronas	2	1 lap behind	119.073
9	Fisichella	Benetton-Playlife	2	1 lap behind	118.989
10	Verstappen	Arrows-Supertec	2	1 lap behind	118.853
11	Alesi	Prost-Peugeot	2	1 lap behind	117.991
12	Trulli	Jordan-Mugen-Honda	3	1 lap behind	117.530
13	Mazzacane*	Minardi-Fondmetal	2	6 laps behind	115.973

*Retired but assessed because of the distance covered.

R E T I R E M E N T S

Driver	Team	Lap	Reason	Ave. (mph)
Herbert	Jaguar-Ford	49	Suspension failure	118.595
Zonta	BAR-Honda	47	Engine failure	118.747
R. Schumacher	Williams-BMW	44	Mechanical failure	117.307
Gené	Minardi-Fondmetal	37	Mechanical failure	116.626
Button	Williams-BMW	19	Mechanical failure	115.762
Frentzen	Jordan-Mugen-Honda	8	Mechanical failure	100.888
De la Rosa	Arrows-Supertec	1	Accident	–
Heidfeld	Prost-Peugeot	1	Accident	–
Diniz	Sauber-Petronas	1	Accident	–

F A S T E S T   L A P S

	Driver	Time (min)		Driver	Time (min)
1	Hakkinen	1:38.543	12	Verstappen	1:41.104
2	M. Schumacher	1:39.064	13	Trulli	1:41.262
3	Barrichello	1:39.302	14	Alesi	1:41.634
4	Coulthard	1:39.529	15	R. Schumacher	1:41.729
5	Villeneuve	1:40.160	16	Gené	1:41.928
6	Irvine	1:40.292	17	Button	1:42.226
7	Wurz	1:40.312	18	Mazzacane	1:43.147
8	Zonta	1:40.498	19	Frentzen	1:44.557
9	Herbert	1:40.764	20	Heidfeld	–
10	Salo	1:40.896	21	De la Rosa	–
11	Fisichella	1:40.925	22	Diniz	–

F1 Race Calender 2001

Australian Grand Prix	Melbourne	4 March
Malaysian Grand Prix	Sepang	18 March
Brazilian Grand Prix	São Paulo	1 April
San Marino Grand Prix	Imola	15 April
Spanish Grand Prix	Barcelona	29 April
Austrian Grand Prix	A-1 Ring	13 May
Monaco Grand Prix	Monte Carlo	27 May
Canadian Grand Prix	Montreal	10 June
European Grand Prix	Nürburgring	24 June
French Grand Prix	Magny-Cours	1 July
British Grand Prix	Silverstone	15 July
German Grand Prix	Hockenheim	29 July
Hungarian Grand Prix	Budapest	18 August
Belgian Grand Prix	Spa-Francorchamps	2 September
Italian Grand Prix	Monza	16 September
United States Grand Prix	Indianapolis	30 September
Japanese Grand Prix	Suzuka	14 October

Picture acknowledgments

Disclaimer